Designing
Small Gardens

Either we shall want our garden to be an alfresco room in which we may sit, meditate, write, eat and doze; or we shall want it to satisfy our craving to grow, enjoy and make happy, beautiful, interesting and exciting plants. – Christopher Lloyd, *Country Life* (1973)

Designing
Small Gardens

Ian Cooke

THE CROWOOD PRESS

First published in 2011 by
The Crowood Press Ltd
Ramsbury, Marlborough
Wiltshire SN8 2HR

www.crowood.com

British Library Cataloguing-in-Publication Data
A catalogue record for this book is available from the British Library.
ISBN 978 1 84797 290 3

Acknowledgements
Thanks to all those who have stayed awake and responded favourably to my talk of the same name as this book, given over many years to dozens of garden societies. Your enthusiasm has encouraged me to complete this project. My appreciation goes to many people who have allowed me to photograph their gardens and in particular, Mark and Keith, Josie and Geoff, Tony and Gillian and Melissa and Keith. Many thanks to Jenny for showing me her neighbour's small gardens in Derby. And finally thanks again to my partner Philip for his support, pithy comments, correction of my grammar and toleration of my single-mindedness as I completed this text. Supper will be cooked next week!

Picture credits
All pictures by the author except pages 11 and 126 Melissa Scott; pages 110 and 118 Marshalls; and page 116 Rolawn.

Typeset by Jean Cussons Typesetting, Diss, Norfolk

Printed and bound in India by Replika Press Pvt Ltd

CONTENTS

PREFACE

Way back at the beginning of my career I worked as a landscape designer, creating small London gardens, terraces, courtyards, balconies and roof gardens. Over time, I moved on to larger estates. My last job was managing a 500-acre university campus that over fourteen years became my much-loved 'big garden', and I used to joke that I earned my living by 'gardening on a grand scale, at someone else's expense'.

But at the same time I have also lovingly cared for the tiny garden that sits behind my small Nottingham town house, and to me that has been equally special. It's the place where I grow my favourite plants, where I actually get my hands dirty, digging, planting and pruning. Here I can also relax, take my shirt off, sit in the sun, eat and drink outside in relative privacy.

My garden reflects my own interests, the exotic style plants that I enjoy and my love of colour. I have lots of exotic looking species, spiky architectural plants, big bold foliage and in the summer, pots of cannas, bananas and other colourful ephemerals. It's also low maintenance and looks after itself for long spells, when I am busy or abroad. The walls are painted bright terracotta, reminding me of my other home in California. There is a tiny fountain that bubbles over cobbles, and the garden has twinkling lights for night time. As gardens go, it's nothing special but it's *my* small garden and absolutely fulfils the needs I have for my space outside.

Over the years, people visiting my gardens have often asked why I don't grow rhododendrons. The simple answer is that I don't like them. To me they are expensive plants with gaudy flowers for just a few weeks each year, but they sit and sulk for the rest of the year in their drab green, and if they don't get perfect conditions they easily become sickly. Now that is of course a bigoted description of a huge genus that gives pleasure to many gardeners, but therein is the uniqueness of gardening. Walk down any suburban street and you are unlikely to find even two gardens that look alike or are growing the same plants. Gardens are very personal creations and express the interests, likes and dislikes and often the personality of the creator. And it is because of this that so many gardens are unique and wonderful.

This book is all about big ideas for small gardens – ideas for new gardens or for improving old ones. You may have moved into a new house with a completely blank plot that needs the full works to create a new garden. But others will have an existing garden that's perhaps looking a bit tired and needs a lift to give it some fresh new interest. It may quite simply be that you have a border that is past its best and looking a bit jaded. Possibly for the first time you have spare cash to spend on a proper garden makeover. Gardeners in all these situations can benefit from these ideas for inspiration.

Most of all I hope that this book will show you how to create the perfect plot in the smallest of spaces.

OPPOSITE: **Bold foliage and bright colours from exotic species challenge the chilly UK climate and fill the author's tiny jungle-like garden.**

1 WHAT DID YOU HAVE IN MIND?

As you are reading this book, I can assume that you have an interest in gardening in its broadest terms. However there are various different types of gardeners. You may be the sort of person that likes a beautiful garden and enjoys plants but doesn't want to spend too much time gardening, preferring to sit and enjoy your garden. Nothing wrong with that! By contrast, others may be the sort of gardener who prefers activity; planting, weeding, pruning and generally working to perfect your garden. You will get immense satisfaction from constantly pottering about, and if you do sit down to look at the garden you will probably soon see an errant twig that needs pruning and have to jump up to deal with it. Such different approaches to gardening will dictate a different slant to design, the style of garden and the plants growing there. Both can be equally successful and rewarding for their owners.

There may of course be other factors. For example you may have a young family, so the garden has to be a safe and secure play environment. Many people will have other interests. I once had two neighbours: one of them filled his garden with pens for the many different breeds of chicken that he kept, and the other was a golf enthusiast who kept the centre of his garden totally open so that he could practise his golf shots. Maybe not exactly gardening, but both were certainly acceptable uses for a garden. Alternatively for those approaching old age, you may need to look at ways of making a garden easier to maintain.

OPPOSITE: **This tiny garden building, possibly once a traditional privy, is now clothed in climbers, making a charming garden feature and very practical storage space.**

Many people who move house initially spend most of their money and time on making the interior of the house comfortable and decorating to their own taste, but really it should be the garden you tackle first. Gardens take time to settle down, grow and mature, so ideally with a new property your garden should be a priority job. Being realistic, most people will inevitably want to replace an outdated kitchen or an insanitary bathroom before spending cash on garden features, but there is a compromise – try to create an outline plan of your new garden, and if at all possible carry out the important planting such as trees, specimen shrubs and climbers; these can be growing while you deal with indoors. Then maybe a year or so later you can come back to the garden, deal with more cosmetic planting and add things like paving and a new lawn, which gives instant effect. Decorative items such as furniture and garden art can be purchased as and when cash is available.

BEING YOUR OWN DESIGNER

Many of the most successful gardens over the centuries have been created by amateur gardeners with a true love of plants and landscapes, who have thoughtfully and lovingly crafted beautiful gardens. Professional garden designers undoubtedly have many skills and are often artistic and innovative, but their approach will always be that of the third-party working for the garden owner and trying to achieve for them the ideal garden. Sometimes when a designer conscientiously creates a beautiful design it can be very disappointing if it's just not what the garden owner had intended.

When you design your own garden, you are

able to define exactly what it is that you want, to mould it into a layout that gives you those objectives, then monitor the process of creating, planting and growing your garden over a number of years. Such a process gives a focus and continuity that is likely to give you a high degree of success and satisfaction. In that way all gardeners are acting as their own designers, day by day and year by year as they improve their gardens.

Creating a beautiful garden of any size does require thought, although it is not essential for you to be a trained draughtsman or a landscape designer. Designing a garden is a process that starts in your mind, where you imagine what the end result will be like and weave together ideas, thoughts and memories into your ideal garden. Some people actually 'think on paper', and drawing plans and small sketches helps them develop their ideas; but to others a plan is as confusing as a map of the New York subway. Rest assured, you only need to put your thoughts on paper as a plan if it helps you with the planning process or you need to communicate those ideas to someone else who will be involved in making the garden.

Dream Gardening

Start by dream gardening – a fun winter activity! Sit down with a glass of wine or a cup of tea and think about all those things you'd love to have in your ideal garden. It may help to make a list as your thoughts develop. Maybe use some books or magazines to stimulate ideas. What would you really like to have?

Perhaps you've always dreamed of an English cottage garden, just like grandma's in your childhood memory. Or you'd like to develop your love of wildlife by creating a garden that will attract birds, butterflies and insects. Maybe you've always wanted fresh vegetables and herbs to use in your kitchen. Perhaps you hate mowing the lawn and would like an alternative surface? Lots of colour maybe, a collection of winter heathers, some scented plants or a collection of exotic

Successful planting schemes need a skilful combination of clear colours and bold shapes, plus matched flowering periods for contrasts such as these.

A cosy table and chairs sheltered by lush planting, just right for a quiet summer breakfast in the sunshine or dinner for two on a warm evening.

foliage and your own palm tree. What's your favourite colour – do you just love blue plants, maybe? And of course it's possible that, much as you love gardens, you hate gardening and want a quiet green oasis that will look after itself.

Don't restrict yourself – put everything that occurs to you on your wish list. Being realistic, there will be some things such as tennis courts and Olympic size swimming pools that you won't be able to accommodate, but it's equally amazing how much can be integrated into a small space if it is carefully planned. For example if you always admired rock gardens full of alpine plants, you could consider a raised bed or an alpine sink. Such a tiny growing area complete with rocks and gravel scree will actually accommodate quite a few alpine plants, spring bulbs and tiny pine trees. Knowing what you want is a very good starting place for any new garden.

The idea of a delicious meal and a few drinks with good friends in the garden on a warm

summer's evening is an attractive proposition for many people. However, the weather in a temperate climate sadly limits the possibility of it happening often, although some gardeners will be willing to invest in the necessities to make it an option. A table and chairs is the obvious minimum requirement. Barbeques come in every size and complexity, from small and portable to shiny and sophisticated like small gas-powered ovens. If you want to stay with traditional charcoal then a built-in brick barbeque can be made as part of the landscape. Probably an outdoor kitchen is beyond the needs of most of us, but it is becoming a common garden feature in warmer climates, complete with cooking facilities, fridge, freezer and running water.

In a temperate climate you will probably be more concerned about the comfort of your guests, and prefer to invest in some heating. Space heaters, like leggy mushrooms, powered by bottled gas are a readily available way of providing localized warmth. Or you may prefer a chiminea – a traditional terracotta wood-burning stove with its own short chimney. On a more sophisticated level a fire pit can be a striking feature with flickering flames providing welcome warmth on a chilly night.

Now if you want to consider real indulgence, what about a hot tub? The so-called portable ones are not outrageously expensive to install and are amazingly cheap to run. In their raw state some tend to look rather 'plastic' but can be built into the landscaping or clad with stone. Sitting in warm bubbling water, with a glass of wine, gazing up at the stars is a magic experience!

Brilliant orange gaillardias contrasted by vivid blue anchusa, photographed in a large garden but equally effective as a small group in a tiny space.

Collecting Ideas

Spend time gathering ideas. There are very few design concepts that are totally new, so don't be afraid to blatantly borrow other people's ideas. Adapt them, improve them or change them to fit your own garden and personal requirements. Few gardeners will object if you adapt a concept from their plot to use in your own. Inspiration is all around us for garden design. Take a walk round the local streets and see what other people have done. As well as noting what appeals to you, make a mental note of things you don't like and the schemes that fail.

Visit gardens open to the public. The Royal Horticultural Society gardens at Wisley, Rosemoor, Hyde Hall and Harlow Carr will show you all that's best in gardens and plants, including small model gardens. There are also numerous gardens open each week under the National Gardens Scheme, advertised in what is known as 'The Yellow Book'. Here you will find big and small gardens, and often communities that will open a series of small gardens in a street or village.

Don't disregard large gardens as inspiration for your small plot. Most big gardens are divided into smaller areas or 'rooms', often with an individual feel or theme. All gardens will have materials or features that may give you ideas. Note anything such as garden furniture, patterns in the paving, containers or combinations of different plants that are particularly effective. You might look at a huge sweeping border of herbaceous perennials but be especially attracted to a particular group of plants. Note the key species and translate it into a small cameo in your own garden.

The Chelsea Flower Show needs no introduction to most gardeners, but in recent years a whole string of garden shows have developed around the country, mostly run by the Royal Horticultural Society. All will display a wealth of new plants piled high in the marquees, and rows of immaculate prize-winning show gardens. Show gardens are inevitably small in size and thus ideal to demonstrate what is possible in a tiny space. However, they will inevitably be seasonal, displaying only what is in bloom at that time. Such events are often horticultural theatre, created to entertain, but they will also be full of ideas you can take away and recreate in your own garden. They are also a valuable source of information. If you see a plant you like, you can often talk to the nurseryman who has produced it and who will tell you all about where and how to grow it. Most shows will also have plants for sale, although this is not so at the Chelsea Flower Show.

Then of course we live in a media age. Each week, TV gardening programmes will give us the idea of the moment, sadly often strongly influenced by some quirky celebrity presenter. Worth watching, but consider some of the more outlandish ideas with caution. The internet is a vast source of information – use Google and you can find any number of ideas for gardens of all sizes. And if you are techie-minded, you can download software to design your small garden on your computer screen, and then view your design as a three-dimensional image.

A notebook is fairly essential for gathering ideas. Make notes of plants you've seen that you'd like to obtain. Jot down ideas, colour schemes, notes on products you like, anything that would jog your memory at a later stage when you are designing your own garden. Leaving the notebook open with special items underlined just before your birthday can be very profitable!

A camera is even better. See something you like, take a picture, and you have a permanent reminder of what you saw to inspire you in your own garden. Whenever you visit a garden show or anywhere else where the plants are labelled, make a point of photographing the label so that when you get back home to import your photographs, you can correctly label the individual plants and know what to look for at a later stage.

A typical contrived flower show garden but full of ideas for colour schemes, plants, materials and accessories for a small paved garden.

Planning on Paper

If you decide to design your garden on paper, the starting point must always be a survey of the site. Start by sketching a rough outline of your garden on a sheet of paper. You should include the outline of the house, the position of any doors or windows, and any other buildings such as garages or sheds. Also mark in any other features that need to remain, such as trees, existing footpaths or paving. There may also be problems that you will have to work around, such as inspection covers, oil tanks or tree stumps. Mark them all on your survey roughly where they appear to be.

You will then need to take some measurements, and for this it can be useful to have a 25m surveyor's tape; you can use a smaller household tape, but it's just going to take longer. Initially measure the boundaries of your garden and then measure and locate all the key features. With an odd shaped garden it can be useful to take measurements as triangles. So for example if you have a tree in the middle of the garden you could measure the length of the fence opposite it and then the distances from each corner to the tree, creating a triangle, which should place it accurately on your page. Where there are a number of features on a straight line, such as windows and doors in a wall, it is often easier to take running measurements, which simply means that you start measuring from one end of the wall and then note the point on the tape at which each window and door starts

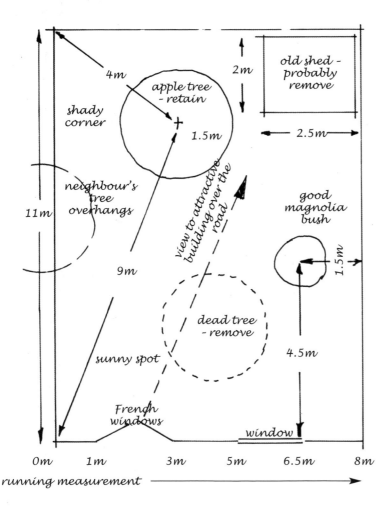

An initial garden survey showing the rough plotting of existing features, some problems and the dimensions of the site, ready for drawing up to scale.

A wide range of materials have been used to construct this beautiful small garden, which is completed with muted planting including the tall *Verbena bonariensis*.

and finishes and you can transfer such measurements easily to your scale plan.

It is worthwhile also noting on your plan anything outside the garden which will influence your design. So for example, note any ugly views that can be seen from the garden that you want to screen, and equally anything attractive that you don't want to hide. If you are lucky enough to have a view from your garden out to the countryside then this is something to frame and use in your design. Even if it's only a pleasant tree on the footpath alongside your garden or a view to a church steeple over the road, this can easily become a valid part of the new garden picture you are creating.

Also you need to know where the sun rises and sets, giving an indication of the sunny and shady

spots. If this is a garden you have worked in for a number of years you will know its idiosyncrasies. You will know the warm spots, the shady corners, the wet spots and maybe places where it's difficult to grow anything. These are sometimes called microclimates.

For the plan itself, landscape designers usually work on a material called drafting film, which is like a thick greaseproof paper, and they will use drafting pens of different thicknesses with indelible ink. Unless you are working professionally there is no reason why you cannot work with a sheet of ordinary paper and pencils. You may find it useful to use squared paper, which will help with drawing to scale. When you have a final design, you can ink it in or make photocopies. For most small private gardens a sheet of A3 paper will probably suffice, although for bigger gardens you may have to obtain a larger size such A2. If you are likely to be working on your design for some time, you may wish to purchase a small drafting board with a built-in sliding ruler, which will give straight edges and accurate right angles. But if this is just a one-off design you can work quite conveniently on a clear surface such as a worktop, with the paper fixed down with sticky tape over the corners.

You will need to work to a scale, in order that your drawing is of the right proportions and that you can calculate materials and plants needed to complete the garden. You can buy scale rulers or simply take a strip of stiff card and transfer measurements from a ruler and mark them up in the correct scale.

A scale of 1:50 or 1:100 will be suitable for drawing most small gardens. 1:100 is a draughtsman's way of saying that 1cm on paper will represent 1 metre on the ground (i.e. 1/100 of a metre). 1:50 means 2cm represents 1 metre (i.e. 1/50 of a metre). Decide what scale you need to use by looking at the largest dimension of your

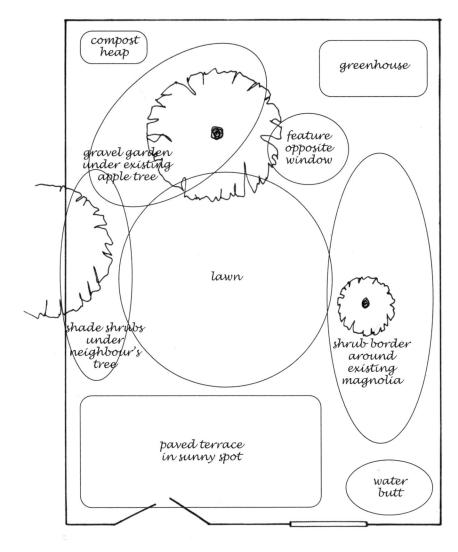

compost heap

greenhouse

gravel garden under existing apple tree

feature opposite window

lawn

shade shrubs under neighbour's tree

shrub border around existing magnolia

paved terrace in sunny spot

water butt

A sketch plan like this is a useful way of starting the design process, by simply locating uses and features before the design becomes detailed.

garden and making sure that this will fit within the longest side of your paper.

Draw out the outline of your garden by scaling up the dimensions from the notes you have taken. Then add in the various features, problems and other factors that need to be considered. This is then the basic outline of your new design on which you can build. It may be useful at this stage to ink in all these factors that cannot be altered, so that when you then start to sketch in your garden in pencil, the essential information will not be lost if you rub out pencil lines. If you have no idea of how you want to plan your garden, use a sheet of tracing paper or kitchen greaseproof paper, over your scale plan so that you can doodle and play with designs without messing up your scale outline.

There are many different ways in which designers work to create new layouts. You might already have some idea where you want to see certain elements of the garden, so for example you might know that the area immediately outside the house is a sunspot in early evening, just perfect for a relaxing paved seating area. Just mark this on the plan in general terms. Perhaps you want to grow shade loving camellias and so you might mark the spot for these under the edge of an existing tree. If you need a path from one part of the garden to another you could mark on an arrow or a loose line to suggest roughly where such a path might go but at this stage don't attempt to draw out precise shapes or dimensions. Some people find it helpful to cut out small shapes for major items such as sheds, greenhouses, trees or seats and then juggle these around until you get a satisfactory arrangement. Such general planning helps leading on to the later stages where we will actually create shapes and pleasing spaces within our garden.

DON'T FORGET TO INCLUDE THESE...

Equipment and Storage

So far you have considered all the attractive aspects of your new garden. But gardens have to serve many purposes and include other essentials that take up space but may not contribute to the desired effect.

You'll need space for dustbins. Many local authorities provide several – one for general waste, one for recyclables and another for garden waste – all highly logical, but they take up space and are not attractive. Or you might opt to make your own compost and plan for a compost bin. You can make your own bin, or there are various proprietary containers. Most will take up at least a square metre of your precious garden, and to effectively make compost you really need two bins, one that you are filling and one that's rotting for use.

You may need a shed for storing all those outdoor things – bicycles, tools, garden chairs, DIY tools and all the rest. When space is very restricted, you might like to consider the smaller wardrobe sized tool stores that take just the essentials. With the widespread use of tumble driers, outdoor space for drying washing is less important, but you may be one who likes to use the sun's heat and so space for a washing line may be necessary. And if you want to be conscientious and recycle water, you will need space for a water butt. There may be other interests that you have that take up garden space, such as pets, chickens, sports or motorbike maintenance.

Gardens for families with small children will also have particular needs. Play items such as swings, climbing frames, slides and sand pits all take up space and need to be carefully integrated into a small garden in a safe way. Obviously the needs of small children will shape a garden at an early stage. As children grow the demands of a family garden will change, and open space with room for ball games will probably become more important.

What You've Decided to Keep

Some of the most difficult gardens to design are those which are total blank sites with nothing in existence. It might seem that such a blank canvas would be ideal for a designer but in fact there is nothing to build a new design around.

Old gardens can be treasure troves for weathered bricks, small pieces of architecture and even simple useful items like these old garden tools.

At the survey stage, you will have already noted any major trees, walls and paths. Also mark on the site any changes in level, contours, steps or retaining walls. You might even have an existing feature such as a garden pool, around which a new design might be built. A structure such as this would be expensive to clear and could well be the focus of a totally new garden.

Consider the condition of any existing lawn, particularly if it covers the area that you would like to be lawn in your new design. An overgrown and neglected lawn can be renovated, providing it was originally good. A renewal process involving cutting, scarification, feeding and weed control should bring a neglected lawn back to a pristine condition within a season and save considerable expense.

Make a thorough inventory of anything in the garden that might possibly be of use in a new design. Note all existing trees, any specimen shrubs, any climbers or shrubs that look reasonably attractive or successful. Remember that a poorly shaped tree that has taken many years to grow can be pruned, shaped or thinned. Equally be prepared to be ruthless with a tree that swamps a garden. Far too often forest or parkland trees such as ash, horse chestnut or sycamore end up in tiny gardens where they impoverish the soil and cast dense shade, rendering a small garden almost unusable. Leyland's cypress is another nightmare tree that should never be in small gardens. Such trees have to go, if you are to create a vibrant new design.

Look also for any useful materials that can be

reused. Older gardens tend to be treasure troves with regard to building materials. You may find lovely old York stone, blue stable bricks, fancy path edgings, terracotta flower pots, garden urns or elaborate pieces of cast-iron from old garden seats or Victorian glass houses. It's amazing what can be hidden amongst the overgrown grass of a neglected garden. Such items can often be reused in a new design. It's a good basis both with trees, plants and materials not to dig out or throw away anything that might be useful until you see how the garden design is developing. By all means clear away the rubbish if the garden is overgrown, and this will enable you to see the clear bones as you plan your new design – but be cautious and do this in stages.

Old-fashioned mop-head hydrangeas are indicator plants, as the flower colour exhibits as either blue or pink according to whether the soil is acid or alkaline.

Gardeners wishing to grow tender exotics like these will need a sheltered garden that is not prone to frost damage or exposed to wind.

WHAT PLANTS CAN YOU GROW?

Understanding Your Soil

A very basic but not particularly exciting aspect of planning your garden is understanding your soil. It's no good dreaming of a garden full of beautiful heathers, camellias and rhododendrons if your soil is chalky and alkaline. Quite simply they won't grow.

Firstly you need to assess the texture of the soil, which is a measurement of its basic components. In simple terms, if the soil feels gritty between your fingers then it is likely to be a sandy soil. If you moisten some of the soil and rub it between your fingers, you will also be able to feel whether it is sticky, which indicates the presence of clay. A good mixed soil will have a balance of sand, silt and clay and is then usually called a loam. Sandy soils tend to be well drained and warm but dry

out quickly in hot weather in the summer. By contrast clay soils are wet, heavy to cultivate but tend to stay moist in dry weather. (Both types are improved by adding organic matter.)

You will also need to know whether your soil is acid or alkaline, and this is measured on a scale called pH. Garden centres will have simple kits that you can use to assess the pH of the soil. A neutral soil, that is neither acid or alkaline, will be around pH 7.0 which is a good level for growing many things. Plants such as rhododendrons will need an acid soil which will have a pH below 7.0. Chalky soils will have a high pH, and in this situation you must carefully choose plants that are tolerant of chalk.

As well as these basic criteria for soils, there may be other matters that will affect a soil's value for growing plants and creating a garden. For example gardens of many new housing developments will have a thin skim of topsoil, often covering rubble and rubbish, under which is a layer of very heavily compressed soil that has been driven over by machines and vehicles during the construction period. Such a compacted and badly drained soil will be a very poor basis for a new garden. You must correct these issues by good cultivation and improved drainage if you want a great garden.

Good garden soils should also be rich with organic matter, which is often indicated by a darker colour and crumbly fibrous texture. Gardens linked to older houses which have been cultivated for many years often have poor worked-out soils. In this situation it is essential to add lots of organic matter, such as compost or manure to improve the soil and restore the soil's life.

Plants to Address Problem Areas

If you are lucky, your garden may be sheltered and warm. But on the other hand it may be cold and exposed. If so, you will need to consider planting tough plants to act as a windbreak, and over time your garden will become more sheltered and warmer. Remember that in winter, cold air will tend to roll downhill and accumulate at the base. This is called a frost pocket, and you will need to choose very tough plants for this situation.

You might also have the problem of noise from a nearby road. Planting a dense shelter to screen out the noise seems the logical answer, although the effectiveness of this is not proven. In practice it seems that if you cannot see the source of the noise, its effect is at least modified, so it's worth trying.

KNOW YOUR LIMITS

Before you embark on a major landscape scheme, do also consider any other restrictions involved in such a project. Constructing and maintaining a beautiful garden can take an inordinate amount of time. Of course creating a garden takes time, but the amount of time needed to maintain it can be controlled by how you design the garden. You can quite easily design a low-maintenance garden

that takes only an hour or so of work a week. Equally if you have plenty of time to spend on your garden you may wish to plan on something more elaborate.

Cash is always a restriction and may curb your more ambitious ideas, but gardens can be constructed in stages, adding the more costly aspects as time goes on. Planning is the key here.

Patience is also a controlling factor. Some of you may be wonderfully patient and be happy to wait for slow growing shrubs to mature and give you a perfect display in a few years. On the other hand many people will see a garden in shorter terms. If you want an 'instant' garden you will need to choose faster growing plants and position them closer together for a quick effect.

Plastic garden stores although useful are not particularly attractive, but they can be easily hidden behind cane screening and luxuriant growth.

2 THE DESIGN TAKES SHAPE

Gardens are very individual expressions of personal interests and what each person finds satisfying. It is likely that in considering your dream garden you have imagined styles or themes that you appreciate and would like to explore in your new garden. Undoubtedly some of these ideas will have come from other gardens you have admired. There are many possibilities, few of which are new and unique but all of which can be explored in your own way in your garden.

GARDEN STYLES

Style is all about how you want your garden to look, but this should also relate to your house and to the local neighbourhood. Sometimes the prompts are obvious – an eighteenth century cottage just calls out for a cottage garden, whereas a stark modern house will suggest a minimalist garden. A city centre property would suggest something formal, whereas a rural location with a view across the fields would prompt for an informal garden that almost flows into the countryside beyond. Local materials may also help, and there might be a local quarry or history of slate working, giving ideas for stone to use in the garden. Maybe a seaside location would inspire you to use driftwood, seashells and bric-a-brac washed up after a high tide. The garden should be an extension of your house and fit gently into the environment. However there can be occasions when the element of surprise can be used; it is an exciting experience to walk into a small enclosed garden and find something totally unexpected.

Plant-Based Styles

Some styles may be based on particular types of plant. For example you might enjoy exotic gardens filled with big bold foliage, palms, bamboos, bananas and bright flowers – all the razzle-dazzle of your own little jungle in your back garden! Others may want something softer, such as prairie style planting which attempts to mimic the vast sweeping wastes of North America with ornamental grasses and herbaceous perennials all growing together in a jumbled confection of soft colour and movement. Some gardeners may wish to specialize in particular plants. You may wish to create a woodland garden filled with rhododendrons, camellias, spring bulbs and other shade loving species. By contrast the rose lover will want a garden that is open and sunny to give the ideal conditions to grow perfect roses. Some gardeners collect particular plants and so the entire garden might be filled with one type of plant; any others would merely be present to enhance the effect of the collection. Whole gardens can be planted in your favourite style so that you can walk through and appreciate the plantings at close quarters.

In all of these examples – and there could be many more – the style of garden is dictated by the plants and the conditions in which they like to grow. Plant lovers' gardens are generally designed for people who enjoy working in their plots. They like collecting and growing certain plants, and the pleasure is not so much in sitting and staring but rather in getting up close and personal with the plants themselves.

OPPOSITE: **Modern designs such as this use a variety of materials like these ornamental timber spindles in innovative ways, all complemented by bold colourful planting.**

Site-Specific Styles

Other garden styles, although distinct, will be less dependent on specific plants. Cottage gardens for example will contain almost anything – shrubs, roses, herbaceous perennials, bulbs, and mixed in amongst them edible plants such as soft fruit and vegetables. In general the plants will tend to be quite simple, and old-fashioned cultivars are often selected rather than the latest novelty plants. This style will also be based on simple materials such as wattle fencing, rustic arches, old York stone paving and traditional garden furniture. A cottage garden looks absolutely perfect surrounding a traditional cottage in a village location. It all goes together perfectly, particularly if you can include a touch of heritage from some older items such as containers from a reclamation yard. Although clutter is generally not a wise idea in any garden, cottage gardens are quite rightly often embellished with a variety of bric-a-brac, pots, ornaments, bird baths and so

on. Cottage gardens are very comfortable; they tend to bring back memories of our childhood or of past holidays, and they're the sort of places where you want to sit and quietly unwind after a busy day.

By contrast, modern architecture demands gardens of a totally different style. Such gardens need to be much more sleek and will probably be geometric and formal, although not essentially so. Many modern gardens are quite minimalist and stark with clear open spaces and distinctly contrived planting. Surfaces will probably use modern materials such as block paving, decking and gravel, and materials such as stainless steel will be used for seats and containers. Planting will feature architectural plants with spiky outlines or bold foliage and solid blocks of planting such as grasses, evergreens, bamboos and ground cover. Not a lavender or rambler rose in sight! Such gardens will tend to be quite visual and make a bold statement but are less likely to have a cosy relaxing feel about them.

This modern garden is formal and geometric, makes good use of colour on the vertical surfaces and is complemented by soft lush planting.

The archway in this garden frames the view to a second area with the carefully sited white stemmed birch, enticing the visitor to explore further.

Using a circular lawn such as this, with good strong surrounding planting, creates a circular space and totally masks the actual shape of the original plot.

STYLE CONCEPTS

Cottage garden: cosy, chintzy
Woodland glade: pastels, greens
Formal parterre: clipped box, yew
White garden: green, white
Exotic garden: bold, leafy jungle
Desert garden: gravel, succulents
Japanese garden: bamboos, raked sand
Mediterranean terrace: sun, colour
Water garden: cool, lush, restful
Summer colour garden: cheerful
Romantic retreat: quiet, peaceful
Minimalist landscape: architectural
Sculpture garden: green setting for art
Heather garden: tiny Scottish glen

A PICTURE POSTCARD OR AN EXPEDITION?

In some circumstances you may want to create a garden that is good just to look at from one particular viewpoint. This might simply be the view from a particular window or from your favourite chair sitting inside a sunroom. In this situation you are aiming to create an image out of plants and other garden materials. It probably doesn't matter whether there is room to wander through the garden, to sit in it or whether it looks good from other positions, as it's just a garden picture. Positioning of the individual plants and components will be quite critical to make sure that the picture is perfect from that all-important viewing point. It doesn't matter if the end of the garden is a muddle or if much of the planting doesn't look right from the far side. Front gardens are a little bit like this, in that they are generally designed to look good from the road as people pass by and as a setting for your house.

However, most people will want a garden that they can experience and explore. The design of such gardens is a little bit more difficult because it has to look attractive from a variety of different angles and also to stand up to close scrutiny as you wander round enjoying the sights. Any groups of plants need to look good from several angles, and island borders will need to have more than one front. In turn this does enable you to be more creative with your plantings. For example you might have a border with the specimen black bamboo, *Phyllostachys nigra* in the centre. This is complemented on one side by a plant of the golden leaved *Choisya* 'Sundance' and on the other side by group of silver leaved *Euphorbia wulfenii*. Both will give different effects that, because of the height and density of the bamboo in the centre, will not be seen at the same time. Having a garden to explore also gives you the opportunity to create little secret hidden areas which are revealed only as you walk down the garden and pass through a hedge or around a trellis. This secret view might quite simply be a splendid pot overflowing with summer colour, or it could be a little corner with a seat just for you to enjoy a quiet cup of coffee.

CREATING DIFFERENT SHAPES

A garden is like a room without a ceiling or a box without a lid. Most gardens attached to small houses are rectangular, but that doesn't mean to say that our garden has to exactly mirror the shape that we start with. Creating an exciting garden is not just about growing plants but also about creating interesting spaces and shapes. Spaces within a garden, like a home, can have different uses: spaces to relax, to play, to entertain, to grow and to do the mundane essentials. Each different space should have a specific feel to it, and this is defined by its design and the materials used.

The curving path leads the eye through the garden, past the colourful planting and towards the slender sculpture in the blue niche.

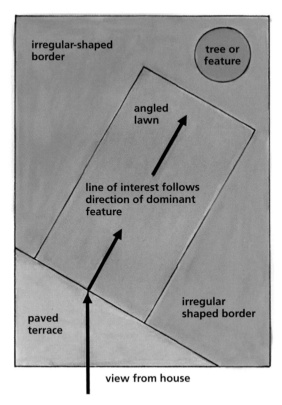

irregular-shaped
border

tree or
feature

angled
lawn

line of interest follows
direction of dominant
feature

paved
terrace

irregular
shaped border

view from house

This diagram shows how placing a shape such as
a rectangular lawn at an angle to the boundaries
turns the emphasis and leads the eye to the tree
at the bottom corner of the garden.

You can very quickly alter the feeling of a
garden by creating a different shape. Let's say you
create a circular lawn within a rectangular garden;
this immediately alters the character of the space,
and the overriding shape becomes a circle. Add
planting around that circumference which
follows its shape and emphasizes its curve, and
the garden immediately becomes a circular
garden regardless of its territorial boundaries.
Creating different shapes in a garden is so much
easier than altering the shape of a room indoors,
but it can have a quite profound effect.

You can also make the shape of the garden
more interesting by altering the axis. This means
that instead of following the boundaries of the
garden with any straight lines or shapes that are

used, you quite simply turn them at an angle.
This works most readily with long thin gardens.
So for example imagine that you need a path
from one end of the garden to the other. Most
people would naturally parallel this to one of the
boundaries, which is uninteresting and makes the
garden look even narrower. In such a situation,
take the path across on the diagonal, and this
immediately leaves you with two interesting
triangular shapes to work with.

Should you want a formal lawn in a rectangular garden, then take the shape of the lawn and
twist it away from the boundaries of the garden.
Immediately the garden becomes more interesting, as your eye is caught by the shape of the lawn
and then turned towards the direction in which
the rectangle points. At the same time the
remaining shapes around the lawn will be a series
of different sized triangles, which will make interesting planting areas – much more appealing than
the narrow thin borders that would have been left
if you had put a rectangular lawn set symmetri-
cally within the boundaries. You can also do the
same sort of thing with curved shapes like ellipses
or even informal shapes. In the simplest terms it
means turning the shapes away from what would
seem to be the logical way of setting them within
the boundaries. Remember that whenever you
turn the axis of a garden it will lead the eye in a
different direction, and this gives fresh opportunities for new features wherever the view leads.

Whether the axis of your garden follows its
outline or if you twist the axis, you can also add
in a cross axis. This will mean another line of
sight that goes across the garden from one side to
the other, crossing the main axis. This would
generally only be discovered as you venture down
the garden. Such a secondary axis may be another
footpath, or possibly a view from a seat to a
garden feature or tree. It is little surprises like this
that make gardens exciting. Logically an axis in
garden design should be straight, but you can also
use gently curving lines and shapes, which will
still lead the eye and interest to another point.

Be careful that axes do not divide up a garden
into too many parts or create shapes that are not
pleasant. You can have an axis that leads the eye

across a lawn to another feature without breaking the lawn up with a path. Use a seat to position the viewer or frame the view with an archway or gap in the planting to direct the eye.

In all of your shapes, it is important to create a balance between open space and bulk – the things that fill your garden, whether trees, plants, furniture or works of art. In particular it is important to keep plenty of open space in a small garden to avoid it feeling cramped. If possible link with other open spaces, such as a view into another garden or the countryside beyond. This can be by way of arches or simply garden windows in a fence.

Small gardens may have only one or two shapes within them, but larger gardens may have a number of shapes. Each individual component that we add to a garden – lawns, paved areas, paths, water features and borders – will have its own shape. The way in which these shapes interact and link with each other has a powerful influence on the success of your garden design. Create good shapes and your garden is almost bound to be successful, whatever the planting may be. However if you just fill a garden with plants and garden features without any consideration for shapes and the layout, the garden is likely to be a confusing jumble.

The shapes in this garden are complex, but the open area in the centre with its mix of paving, grass and water gives a feeling of spaciousness.

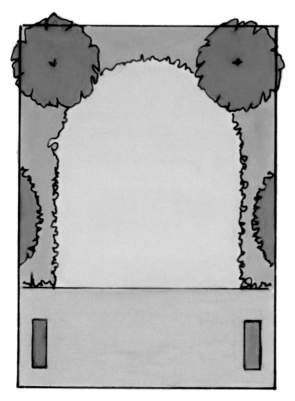 

The top left plan shows a garden which is totally symmetrical, whereas the top right plan shows similar landscape elements which are arranged in a more relaxed but balanced arrangement.

FORMAL OR INFORMAL

Garden designs tend to be either formal or informal. Formal designs are based on straight lines and geometric shapes. The shapes may include curves, but these would be geometric curves that can be constructed using a pair of compasses, such as circles, ellipses, ovals or parts of these. Formal gardens do not have to be symmetrical although they should be balanced, as should any garden design. Symmetry involves having exactly the same on the right-hand side of your garden as you have on the left, basically a mirror image. There may be occasions when symmetry is right, but usually it looks rather too contrived and is not as interesting as a balanced garden. For example a small garden might be based on three rectangles: a large rectangular lawn towards the left-hand side, and on the right-hand side a medium-sized paved terrace (again a rectangle) with a small rectangular pool on the bottom right-hand side. The large shape on the left is balanced by the small and medium shapes on the right.

Informal gardens do not use geometric shapes and are usually based on a series of gently flowing forms and irregular curves that do not fit any fixed pattern. The aim is to create a garden design which is much more natural rather than contrived. Informal gardens are unlikely to be symmetrical and tend to fit more with the cottage garden style, prairie plantings and wildlife gardens. Whenever you use curves within a garden, whether they be parts of a circle or free-flowing lines, be sure to use bold curves.

 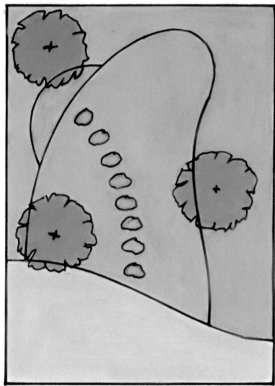

In these two plans the differences between a formal garden with geometric shapes and a more natural informal garden are demonstrated.

These will give a strong emphasis in the design and look exciting. In the simplest terms, the edge of the border with two bold curves will look much more effective than one with five little wiggles.

Although gardens tend to fall into one category or the other – formal or informal – it is possible to mix the two. So for example you might have a long garden that starts off with a formal patio and geometric shaped lawn near the house, and then passes into another area with a different style and a different feel that may be laid out in a more informal way with loosely curved borders and gravel paths. Making the two styles flow gently into each other is part of the skill of the garden designer.

DEVELOPING THE DESIGN

Keep Everything to Scale

It is sometimes difficult to know how to start creating a new design. Earlier on we spoke about marking key existing features on your plan and sketching in the rough locations of things that you might want to include such as a sunny terrace, an open lawn for children's play, room for a vegetable patch and a herb garden near the house.

The next stage is crafting those loose ideas into something more precise: shapes and spaces using various materials. As you try to create shapes that will become your design it can be helpful to use a grid that is prompted by the proportions of the

This tiny but well-planned space includes a seat, a piece of sculpture and a water feature together with exciting planting, a timber fence, climbers and hedging.

house and any other main features in the garden. In this way the components of the garden will be in proportion to the scale of the house.

Careful design is important for all landscapes but particularly so with small gardens where space is at a premium. You cannot afford to waste space with features that are not effective or plants that really don't perform well. It is by thinking through your design carefully that you are most able to fit the maximum into a small space. And although you probably still won't be able to squeeze in a swimming pool or tennis court, you may well be able to achieve far more than you originally thought. In working with small spaces there are various techniques and tricks that will help you to be most successful.

Initially do remember the scale in which you are working. If it's a small space, then match the components of your garden to that space. Use bricks or block paving rather than large paving slabs. This will help to make the space look larger. Choose garden furniture that is at the smaller end of the scale. Don't choose a table and six chairs, if it's just usually you and your partner that dine outside. Choose a nice little intimate table and two chairs and when you have guests, plan a

OPPOSITE: **Adding a curve to this path has given the garden an air of mystery, hinting at further delights to be explored beyond the roses and round the corner.**

buffet or dine indoors. If in doubt try a table and chairs from indoors and see how they fit in the space you have before buying garden furniture.

In a small garden you need to avoid plants that grow too big and take up too much space. Choose small narrow trees and plants which are compact or dwarf. For example a favourite spring flowering shrub is *Forsythia* and the most common cultivar for sale is 'Lynwood' which grows to about 2m (6ft) high and can spread to an unwieldy bush just as wide. In a small garden you would be much better to choose one of the dwarf cultivars such as 'Fiesta' or 'Gold Cluster' which makes a small bush no more than a metre high and wide and still give you a mass of golden spring flowers.

Creating an Illusion

There are various tricks that you can use to make a small plot seem bigger than it really is. One of the simplest is to suggest that there is more of the garden hiding away. So as you plan the position of footpaths, lawns or other open spaces, allow for them to disappear behind a block of planting, a hedge or other screen. As you view the garden, your eye follows the shapes you have created as far as it can; the brain then takes over and concludes that there is more hidden away. In reality, the footpath that winds behind the border may only go to the compost heap, but unless your visitor explores the garden it will always look fascinating! However if you have room, the disappearing path

A painted backdrop such as this is pure theatre in a garden, but surely more attractive and fun than the blank wall that it covers.

can lead to a quiet corner with its own features and interest.

A more complicated deceit involves the use of false perspective. When used in the garden it means making sure that the parts of the garden that are furthest from the house are proportionately smaller than those near the house. So, say you have a garden design that is comprised of three circles; by making the one nearest house the largest, the next smaller and one furthest away the smallest, you will actually make the garden appear as if it is much longer than it really is. You can do the same thing with vertical aspects of the garden. You might want to include a series of clipped evergreen shapes. The ones nearest house could be 2m in height, those further away 1.75m and the ones furthest from the house 1.5m. Providing they are similar in all other aspects this again would suggest that the garden is much longer than it really is. You can use the same principle with many aspects of a small garden.

Whenever possible, divide up the garden into different spaces or rooms. Many quite small gardens are long and thin, and they readily lend themselves to splitting into different areas. Give each room a slightly different style to make the garden more interesting. Your divisions should not totally block the view from one space to the next, because this will have a negative effect and make your garden look smaller. Ideally the visitor should be able to look from one area to the next, getting a progressive view of the spaces to encourage them to explore. Low hedges, trellises, archways and planting in mixed heights will all give a sense of mystery and help to give the illusion that the garden is bigger than it really is.

Using mirrors in a small garden is one specific trick that can be useful. It is sometimes said that mirrors tell the truth in the bathroom but lie in the garden. Ideally use a mirror that is large enough and positioned in such a way that the effect it creates is believable. Mirrors are most effective when they are positioned at an angle from the viewer so that another part of the garden is seen without the reflection of the viewer. If possible set a mirror in a false doorway or arch so that it is conceivable that there is more beyond. Alternatively plant some climbers to mask the edges. Use a good quality mirror and seal the back and edges to help the mirror survive outside.

In a more elaborate scheme some great gardens have used the technique *trompe l'oeil* (meaning fools the eye) to great effect. In its simplest terms, they might paint a blank wall, like stage scenery, to represent something that adds to the effect of the garden. You might try something similar, add painted windows, a false door, or something more intricate such as a statue in a niche or an imagined view to the countryside beyond the garden. It's all down to imagination and how inventive you feel.

3 ELEMENTS OF A GOOD GARDEN

Gardens are generally considered to be places to grow plants, but a visit to any flower show will demonstrate that an amazing range of materials can be used to create exciting gardens. Gardens have floors, walls, furniture and features, as well as beds of plants and flowers. Landscapers will speak of soft and hard landscape. Soft landscape includes lawns and all other areas of growing plants such as trees, borders and planters. Hard landscape refers to paving, walling, and any other constructions such as pools, pergolas and garden buildings.

GROUND SURFACES

In this chapter lawns are considered alongside hard landscape, as lawns also represent one specific option for the ground surface of a garden.

Lawns and Groundcover

Grass is just one of many surfaces that can be both usable and attractive. There are many materials that can be used for your garden floor – don't automatically assume you need a lawn. Consider whether you want a surface that will take wear and foot traffic, or is it just a neutral open space? Grass is a traditional component of many classic gardens and will no doubt be essential if you are creating a cottage garden or other style with a feeling of heritage. Grass is restful to look at and provides a good green foil against which most

other colours can be effectively used. In a family garden, children require play space, and grass is a forgiving material that absorbs many knocks and bumps and also recovers well from damage after games like football. However grass requires constant mowing and ideally other maintenance if you want a good quality lawn.

Grass can be treated in different ways. In very formal gardens, it is often cut short, with a cylinder mower that will leave light and dark stripes. That is a very traditional treatment. Cutting with a rotary mower and leaving the trimmings gives a much more relaxed finish. Interesting effects can be created by mowing different areas of a lawn at different heights, or by cutting a mown path through an area of meadow.

Although flowering meadows undoubtedly look more impressive on a large scale, in a small garden there is no reason why you cannot include a patch of meadowland that will be both good to look at and attractive for wildlife. Good wildflower meadows can be grown from seed or from small plug plants. In general meadows should be left to grow, flower and seed through the early months of the year and then mown in July or August. All the mowings should be removed to encourage the wildflowers to grow again the next year. Never use fertilizers or weedkillers, and your meadow will improve year by year.

Alternatively there are many other groundcover plants that can be used to get a tapestry of green or other colours. Chamomile and thyme are probably the most familiar lawn substitutes (*see* page 130) Both will take limited foot traffic but are not suitable for family gardens and heavy wear. Both will need an annual trim but do not require regular mowing. Weeding will be essential in the early stages whilst new plants are establishing.

OPPOSITE: The striking orange *Heuchera* 'Crème Brûlée' provides a brilliant contrast to the grass in this small space, demonstrating one of the more adventurous alternatives to a plain lawn.

There are many different types of ivy, *Hedera* cultivars, many with coloured foliage and interesting shapes, and all thrive in sun or shade. Ornamental grasses such as *Festuca glauca* and *Hakonochloa macra* 'Aurea' are easy to grow, and the various different types of *Lamium maculatum* will give flower and foliage. Bergenias seem to be 'love or hate' plants, but they are excellent groundcover with early spring flowers and big bold evergreen leaves that contrast well with delicate foliage such as grasses. There are also a number of carpeting junipers such as *Juniperus* 'Emerald Spreader' which makes a carpet of ground-hugging emerald green foliage no more than 10cm tall. There are many other species can be used either on their own or mixed together to create a living carpet.

Some of the most effective small gardens do not use lawns at all but are surfaced with any one of a number of other landscape materials: paving, gravel, cobbles and decking are probably the most familiar. These hard landscaping materials are durable, hard wearing and require minimum maintenance but will be initially expensive. They will usually have to be laid by a professional, or you will have a long and laborious job to complete the work yourself. However it can be very satisfying to do a job such as this, and know that when the work is complete, it's all your own.

Paving

Gone are the days when paving was just concrete slabs in a selection of garish pastel shades. Take a trip to any builders' merchant's and you will find a huge range of paving supplies. The most expensive will usually be natural stone materials. The commonest of these is York paving, a traditional sandstone in shades of buff. Much good sandstone paving is sourced from India and will be available in various rectangular sizes. There is usually a range of different colour variations from light to dark grey, buff, browns and reddish shades often with beautiful striations throughout. There is also a huge market in secondhand York stone paving, which will usually have seen a former life as street paving in a major city. Such secondhand paving has a lovely mellowed look which may be just right for many traditional gardens. However being secondhand does not mean it will be cheap, as weathered York stone is very expensive. The negative side of York stone paving is that when damp in winter it tends to grow algae and become slippery. Other natural stone options, without this problem, are real granite and slate.

Then there will be many different types of manufactured concrete paving slabs. The simplest and cheapest of all will be rectangular grey slabs. Others will have various different colours, and may incorporate different attractive aggregates into the surface. Some have a riven finish that attempts to mimic natural stone, but these are rarely effective. Others have a rough, granular surface that makes them non slippery and can be quite stylish. Some of the most elaborate ceramic tiles look beautiful but will be very expensive and may well be slippery when used outside. Manufactured paving will come in a number of interlocking sizes that can be laid in various different patterns. Most manufacturers will also include matching edgings and specialist items that will create octagonal or circular areas.

In the past, landscapers used bricks for paving, either for whole paths, as edges or to add areas of interest amongst paving. Traditional clay house bricks look lovely when laid as paving but often do not wear well and soon start to disintegrate with the effects of frost and sun. Engineering bricks are harder and last well. The modern hard wearing version is the block pavier, made of tinted concrete. The simplest of these will be the shape and the size of an ordinary brick, but there are now many exciting shapes, sizes and finishes. All of these are relatively small in size in comparison to paving slabs. All sorts of exciting colours and shapes are available, and the possibility for creating interesting paved surfaces is endless. Explore your local builders' merchant's and see which materials you like. Suppliers will often give you samples so you can take home a few block paviers and maybe a broken paving slab to see how the different colours look together in your garden. Do remember that the colour of all concrete products

On this little patio the designer has created an attractive pattern of different tinted and sized paving slabs which have also been used for the steps and for surfacing the seating areas.

Traditional granite sets have been combined in this garden with loose cobbles and simple planting of dicentra and heucheras to surround a tiny rill of trickling water.

fades a little with time, but will usually come back every time there is a shower of rain.

The paving in your garden can be as plain as a berber carpet or as intricate and exotic as a Persian rug. There are so many different paving materials available that can be used in limitless ways. A garden that is packed with exciting plants and a range of eye-catching features will probably need an uncomplicated pattern of paving. By contrast, in a simpler garden you might choose to make the paving itself a feature.

It is generally best to choose one or two types of paving as the basic types, and you can contrast panels of block paving with paving slabs or maybe use different colours. You can make patterns using different shapes and sizes. Most paving manufacturers will offer templates suggesting possibilities. Beyond this there are numerous other materials that can be used as small feature panels within the paving surface, such as granite setts, blue stable bricks, terracotta floor tiles or round cobbles. Do be inventive when planning a new terrace or footpath – the possibilities are endless.

Edgings

Unless there is a good reason, do not emphasize an edge but leave the surface, whether it be grass, paving or soil as a clear statement on its own. There are some truly awful plastic, concrete and metal edgings available which serve no purpose at all. They draw the eye to themselves and detract from the genuine features and materials of the garden.

Some edgings can be effective. If you have a mixed border immediately adjacent to a lawn, there can be problems with plants flopping over the lawn and preventing proper mowing and edging. In this situation, a discrete mowing strip of York stone or other paving, no more than 20cm wide and set at the same level as the lawn, will solve the problem. In a cottage garden, keep-

OPPOSITE: **Various different sized gravels and cobbles have been used here with boulders and slate chippings as a setting for the featured mirror ball and lime green cushion.**

ing gravel separate from soil can be an issue. There are now some very good modern reproductions of the old Victorian clay edgings in both terracotta and blue.

Gravel and Cobbles

Many modern gardens use gravel, which can make a quite striking but economical finish. Gravel is a generic term to describe the many different types of small natural aggregates that are available, usually 10–25mm (½–1in) in size. The most basic of these is pea shingle, which is multi-coloured but tends to fade to a fairly uniform greyish brown. It's cheap and readily available. Golden gravel tends to hold its colour better, retaining a nice warm look. Many others are available from pure white, through shades of grey, bluish greens to black. Red porphyry is distinct

terracotta red and retains its colour well as it weathers. Slate chippings are also available in blue, green and plum.

For interest and contrast add larger pebbles, cobbles, flint rejects or boulders. Again, a host of different materials, colours and sizes is available. Cobbles come loose or bagged, 40–80mm (2–3in) in diameter. Boulders can be almost any size and are usually purchased individually. You can often choose exactly which ones you want. Two or three big boulders will make a better statement than a heap of smaller ones, but do remember that big rocks can be very heavy to handle. Never choose stone that is bigger than you can safely manipulate in your garden with simple equipment such as a sack truck.

Recycled glass is an interesting way to add colour to the landscape. It is available usually in shades of blue, green and sometimes red, and will

This innovative garden combines fountains with metal grille surfacing, and it's a fair guess that the owner would be tempted to turn on the fountains as guests explore the garden!

have been tumbled to remove the sharp edges. The smaller sizes can be used as a surfacing material; it is also available as glass rocks for features and use in outdoor firepits. Although very effective, the larger sizes can be quite expensive.

Metal Grilles

For a really innovative floor surface in a lawn or shallow pond, consider using metal grilles. These need to be built into some sort of framework which holds them above ground level. You can then plant small low-growing groundcover species underneath, so you can walk above them without damaging them.

Alternatively install them over a shallow pond with a fountain, and you have both a water feature and a patio. When the fountain is off, the grilles act as a surface that can be used as a patio, and then when the patio isn't needed, you can turn the fountain on for the full visual effect.

Footpaths

Garden paths can be either boring or quite exciting. At their most mundane, they are no more than a smooth surface that takes you from one end of the garden to the other. You can use any of the materials already discussed, although grass paths tend to wear quickly if they get much traffic. Some sort of paving is usually more effective if paths are going to be heavily used.

Footpaths, whether straight or curved, also lead the eye from one point to another. The end of a footpath is a good place to add a feature, whether it be a seat, a piece of sculpture, or simply a large container of plants. Where your garden is big enough to have different rooms, footpaths can lead through archways, or between gaps in hedges and walls, drawing the eye as well as the visitor to the next area. Footpaths are like signposts in the garden, telling you which direction to both look and walk.

A stepping stone path over a lawn, through borders or even across a pool can be an attractive feature. As a practical path, it will cope with some light foot traffic. As a landscape device, stepping stones provide a gentle indication of direction without totally breaking up the surface and shape of the material, such as grass, that covers the whole area. Stepping stones allow for easy access in a border and provide a fun experience when crossing over water.

LEVELS AND CONTOURS

Having slopes or banks in a garden can initially be seen as a problem, but actually it gives great potential. Gardens that are on more than one plane are far more interesting that those that are totally flat. A small change in level leads to graceful gentle slopes which provide good links in informal designs. Lawns and borders can easily cope with shallow contours and look all the more attractive for them. Providing the slope is not too steep, planting will help to stabilize a bank. Low-growing groundcover plants are particularly successful at this as the roots will colonize the soil, reducing erosion.

Steeper sites will require a more complex treatment, but this can nevertheless become a feature of the design rather than a problem. Steep banks are not conducive to gardening, as the soil tends to wash down in flower beds, sloping lawns are difficult to mow, and obviously you cannot use slopes for paving or gravel areas. So terracing is the best solution for steeper gradients. This simply means reconstructing the slope into a series of level stepped areas. Terraced gardens can be quite stunning, with different levels interacting, steps giving access and planting that is built up at different heights. The garden truly becomes three-dimensional.

The construction aspects of terraced gardens are however complex. Any walls you build to retain the different levels of soil must be quite substantial and well anchored into the slope, as the weight of soil pushing down and out will be considerable. Steps must also be well constructed so that they do not slide down the slope with time. If parts of your terraced garden are to be used for growing then as you level the terraces you must be sure not to bury the topsoil. You will need to 'cut and fill', scraping back the topsoil,

The tiered pools and raised planting in this landscape give the garden a three-dimensional effect, particularly valuable when the garden is new and immature.

levelling each terrace and then replacing the topsoil on the top.

The most expensive form of terracing will undoubtedly be with bricks or concrete blocks, which must be laid on a firm foundation. Walls will probably need to be 20cm (9in) thick with two skins of brick, or usually block inside and brick as the fair face. Walls can also be constructed from timber using materials such as old railway sleepers, wooden stakes or even woven hazel panels, although the flimsier the construction, the less it is likely to retain the soil for any length of time. The use of gabions is gaining popularity. These are wire cages that are positioned where you want your wall and then filled with stone of some sort. Another solution is broken multi-coloured bricks, which can be very attractive, but the whole units can be quite bulky and you will need to consider whether they are worth the space they take.

WALLS AND FENCES

All gardens have boundaries. As well as performing very necessary functional tasks such as marking your property ownership, and keeping your neighbour's children out or your own dog in, they can also become valid parts of the created landscape. Walls and fences will give your garden privacy, help to shape the different spaces you create and also give vertical accents.

If you want privacy, avoid falling into the trap of creating a fence like a fortress. There may be only certain places where neighbours or the public can see into your garden. These are the areas to screen. When neighbours' windows overlook your garden, it may be easier to screen these views with individual trees or tall shrubs. Boundaries can be solid like fences or broken barriers like trellis, which allows a partial view to what is beyond.

The bold leaves of the gunnera in this very masculine garden perfectly complement the rough 'log cabin style' fencing that surrounds the plot.

This simple classical flower pot has become special by painting it just the right colour to match the hint of orange in the colourful leaves of this phormium.

Hedges are green garden walls and relatively cheap to purchase and plant. Once established they will give you a neutral green background against which you can create your garden. Hedges however are not instant barriers, and if you plant small plants it may take five or more years before you have a full-size hedge which will give you privacy and enclosure. Instant hedges are now available from nursery suppliers, but they tend to be expensive.

FOCAL POINTS AND FEATURES

In the nineteenth century, the big estate land-scapes were planned so that visitors went from one point of interest to the next: a ruined temple, a rocky grotto, a rustic bridge, a towering folly and on to a roaring cascade. Even in a tiny garden, we can create a series of interesting features so that a walk round the garden is punc-tuated by a series of highlights. These must be in key locations, either viewed from the house or only visible as we walk round the garden.

Planted containers are often the favoured choice for many gardeners. Containers offer the opportu-nity to create small cameo planting schemes which can be revised once or twice a year. The whole range of summer bedding plants offers a wonderful palette of fast-growing, colourful and exotic look-ing plants. Rotate these with spring bulbs such as tulips and you have first-class material for filling a container and creating a feature. Some gardeners may prefer something more permanent, and ever-greens such as clipped box specimens may strike just the right note in your garden.

The range of containers available is huge, including classical terracotta pots, glazed pottery containers and wooden boxes like the traditional *Versailles Caisse*, originally used for growing citrus trees. Do ensure that any clay pots you select are frost hardy or be certain to take them indoors for the winter. In some cases you may feel a very special container is adequate on its own and acts like a piece of sculpture, without needing embel-lishment of plants. The choice is yours!

Too often, gardeners are happy with the most mundane of tumbledown fences which add noth-ing to the garden. Usually walls and fences are backgrounds rather than main features, but they can still be attractive and contribute to the overall design. Traditional brick walls are lovely to enclose a garden. The mellow terracotta of brick is a good foil for green foliage, and the brick will also retain heat, keeping plants nearby just a little warmer in cold weather. However new brick walls are very expensive to construct.

Various types of concrete block are also avail-able. The most basic is sound and strong, but unattractive and will usually need rendering with cement mortar and finishing with masonry paint. Some 'fair faced' concrete blocks are more orna-mental and available in different finishes which may well be suitable for garden walls. Those that attempt to mimic natural stone with a riven and coloured finish rarely look effective. Avoid them!

Garden furniture of course serves a practical purpose, but in many ways it also acts as a feature

A root feature such as this will not last for ever but provides a great contrast to the accompanying ferns as it gracefully decays beneath its mossy covering.

in your garden. In particular individual seats and benches placed in key locations throughout the garden act as highlights. Some garden artists are designing very special seats that can also be described as sculpture. When positioning a seat, remember that the piece of furniture needs to look good where you place it; equally it must also be positioned so that those using it will have a pleasant view.

The idea of sculpture in your garden may seem a little esoteric to some people, but in this category I would include any sort of artistic item which you find pleasant and can be used as the focal point in your garden. Any garden show will give you all sorts of ideas of the items available, some of which can be very beautiful but often very expensive. However there are inexpensive versions of most of these items, and some of them such as sundials, bird feeders or weathervanes will have a valid purpose as well as being ornamental. Various different obelisks, tripods and wigwams, made of metal, timber or woven hazel twigs can be utilized as garden highlights, either on their own or more often when used as a support for climbing plants such as clematis or climbing roses. They can be painted whatever colour is appropriate in your garden.

Some of the most exciting and often economical garden features can be recycled items. Take a trip to your local salvage yard and you will find all sorts of curious items of architectural and garden heritage. Pieces of carved stone, armless statues, redundant post boxes, ornamental cast iron Victorian chimney pots, agricultural items and a whole host more. Enterprising gardeners might look for stained glass panels, to be fixed where the light will catch them or even to be utilized in a small garden shelter.

A dead tree can also be considered an opportunity. Paint the whole tree, trunk and branches a bright colour and enjoy it as a short-term eye catcher until the branches start to decay and fall. Alternatively some chainsaw users consider themselves artists and may well be happy to create for you a totem pole or unique carving from a dead tree trunk or fallen tree. (Caution: chainsaws are very dangerous and should never be used by amateurs or untrained operatives.) A trip to the beach may also yield attractive items such as stones, shells or driftwood; and the countryside offers mossy logs and upturned roots. Do beware of removing anything from land that is not yours, which could be construed as theft.

Position any features carefully and in a way that they do not conflict with each other. If you place a beautiful specimen shrub next to a cast

GARDEN HUMOUR

Gardens should be fun, and they often express the sense of humour of the creator. Over the years I have seen plastic sheep grazing on a lawn, a topiary Loch Ness monster beside a pool, a battleship clipped from privet, an old washing machine converted to a water feature and plants growing in the most bizarre of containers. Garden gnomes seem to elicit the most scathing of responses, but maybe there's a place for the odd one or two (do be careful as they breed!). Sometimes garden humour can be quite sophisticated, like the beautiful tiny bronze woodcutter, complete with saw, standing precariously on a tree branch that he is in the process of cutting through. And why not, if it raises a smile?

Fortunately the sheep in this garden will not damage the planting or require shearing but will undoubtedly raise a wry smile or two from guests.

iron urn cascading with geraniums and jostling with a bronze Aphrodite all in one area, it will just result in horticultural indigestion! Locate and space your features so that they form a composition and some sort of progression. You might well have some containers of flowers on your patio near the house and easily seen from the windows, then an obelisk with climbers as a feature amongst a bed of perennials further down your garden, and at the end of a key footpath a small piece of sculpture. All of this can be seen as a succession of highlights as you look down the garden. Do also consider the settings for features; the backgrounds and spaces they occupy. A square of good paving or a neatly clipped niche in a green hedge will certainly add to the impact of a feature. The element of surprise is also valuable; it's exciting to suddenly come across something unexpected. So on exploring the garden the visitor may find a little corner tucked away with a quiet seat or simply a piece of weathered driftwood displayed on some old mossy York stone.

The unusual water feature in this garden consists of a shallow sheet of gently flowing water that looks like a rippling mirror as it passes over the black paved surface.

Water Features

Water is probably one of the most powerful elements that you can use in a garden design and is usually high on people's 'want' list when they are thinking about a new garden. Water can be considered as a feature, in that it inevitably attracts the eye as something special. However it can also be considered as a garden surface or texture, very much as we would consider a lawn, paving, walls or even planting. Broad expanses of water act like open spaces in the garden, even if we can't walk on them. A large sheet of still water also acts like a mirror and will reflect surrounding plants, trees or other garden features on its surface. This is particularly so with pools that have been painted black or lined with black butyl. Such pools can act as a perfect mirror on a sunny day.

One variation on a water feature is a natural swimming pond, which combines an ornamental feature with a swimming pool. These pools use gravel, stone and clay in place of concrete or fibreglass, and aquatic plants instead of harmful chemicals and complicated mechanical filtering systems. The result is a relatively inexpensive pool that is beautiful, ecologically diverse and available for swimming.

Moving water is even more dynamic. Movement provides an energy within a garden; a unique sound and an ever-changing pattern as sunlight catches the droplets from a gently jumping fountain or rushing waterfall. Many different types of commercial fountains are available in garden centres, from small jets that bubble over cobbles, through to more spectacular patterns of dancing water and then various clever devices such as granite balls gently revolving on a watery bed. Some of these can be purchased needing little more than plugging in to a suitable outdoor electric supply. Of course you can be more inventive and design your own water feature: buy a basic pump and the necessary pieces of plumbing and construct something unique. Even the tiniest of gardens can have a water feature if you choose and position it carefully.

Waterfalls tend to be more difficult, in that they require two different levels to operate effectively. This will necessitate the construction of an upper and lower pond, and some sort of weir over which the water can cascade in an attractive pattern. The water is then pumped back up to a higher level. The most ineffective waterfalls are those that try to look natural. A tiny rock garden with a concrete channel lined with miscellaneous shaped rocks attempting to look like a Derbyshire rill is unlikely to be effective and most likely to constantly leak. Don't attempt it!

In contrast to the more formal pools, you may wish to construct an informal pool or small stream. This is much more challenging where space is restricted in a small garden. The best natural pools have soft edges where marginal plants can grow in the moist boggy soil. Such pools will be ideal for attracting wildlife, insects, butterflies, frogs and toads and the myriad of small creatures which live within the water of

This little arbour acts as a cosy retreat and a surprise feature amongst the colourful planting, but don't forget to take the cushions indoors before it rains!

such pools. If you want to keep fish, don't be in a rush to add fish to a new pond – let it settle down and become balanced first.

Anyone with small children or small visitors will need to carefully consider the risks associated with any open space of water. Drowning can easily happen with only a few inches of water. Covering over a traditional pond with a steel mesh may be one way of dealing with the problem, but it is rarely the most attractive. A better solution is to create a moving water feature which has no exposed depth of water. Bubbling fountains where the water cascades over boulders and disappears into a hidden underground chamber can be interesting and very safe. Be sure that the lid which covers the reservoir is substantial enough to avoid someone – child or adult – falling through. Some designer fountains with smooth surfaces and sheets of shallow moving water can be very effective, as can fountains that shoot up from a paved surface – great fun for children of all ages and very safe!

Arbours, Arches and Trellises

An arbour is usually a wooden structure with vertical poles and horizontal struts above head height to support climbers. Such features are more important in hot countries where it is necessary to give shade to an outdoor seating area. Pergolas are very similar but will normally be more elongated, covering a pathway. In any garden, you can still use them as a feature. Arches are smaller structures, merely bridging a path. If you decide to include an arch, do make sure it has a clear purpose, perhaps marking the boundary between one garden area and another, or framing the view to something interesting. All of these are quite substantial garden features and so in many ways contribute to the structure of the garden.

Trellises can be very useful as partial boundaries within a garden, where you want to create some height and enclosure but without the solidity of a fence. Trellises can be attractive if they are well made of attractive timber and are usually used as supports for climbers. When well established, the plants will probably take over as

providing most of the boundary. Trellis work can also be used fixed to a wall as a support for a climber. Such panels will primarily be utilitarian, allowing support for a plant, but if well designed can be a feature in their own right until the plants get established. Trellis and fencing may also be needed to hide essentials such as bins or oil tanks. Try to make a well-designed feature out of such disguises, or they will always look like a trellis round an old oil tank.

Garden gates tell us a lot about the garden owner. It may be a gate that allows you to see through and welcomes you to the garden and house, or a solid door that indicates the need for privacy. In some cases it can be quirky and express a sense of humour – a shared joke with passers-by. Gates are not easy to make, so if you want an individualistic gate it is best to start with a ready-made gate and then adapt it to your own style.

Garden Structures

Most small gardens will not have enough space for garden buildings on any scale. Sheds, greenhouses, conservatories and summerhouses will take up a considerable amount of space. If you are considering any of these, think carefully about the essentials and how you can fulfil the needs whilst taking up a minimal amount of space.

Rather than a full-scale summerhouse, you might wish to include a small timber arbour, which can act as a feature and provide a comfortable, sheltered seat – your own special place in the garden. Some utilitarian areas such as bicycle stores, log heaps and waste bin areas can be so designed that they incorporate a feature. The roofs of such areas do not need to be covered with traditional roofing material, but can be constructed as growing areas and planted up with alpine plants or other favourite species.

A variety of small tool stores are available which will give you storage for the basic garden equipment. Remember, if you don't have a lawn you won't need a lawn mower. In a tiny garden a wheelbarrow may not be needed; a pop-up bin takes up limited space when folded up and is ideal for the waste generated by most weeding

The rather impressive classical architecture with its coat of ivy in this garden hides a mundane but quite essential wooden garden shed.

and pruning jobs, and for heavy handling, moving large pots, sacks of compost and paving slabs, a sack truck may be more useful and takes up far less space in storage. If you do decide that you need a garden shed, think carefully how it can be integrated into the garden design and made into an attractive feature with screening or planting.

Conservatories are a blend of indoors and out. They should have enough comfort to suggest indoors and enough horticulture to evoke garden. These are places which should be comfortable on a winter's day so that you can enjoy the garden despite the weather. A good conservatory will have comfortable furniture and a range of plants that will give the feeling of being in the garden. Sadly many conservatories often become a repository for all sorts of bric-a-brac that has no other home and for struggling plants that you are trying to overwinter.

Greenhouses are difficult to integrate into a small garden. To be useful they must be sited where they will get full sun and for easy connection to electricity and water, which often means a prominent location. Inevitably the glare of the glass will make the structure appear dominant whenever the sun shines, and few greenhouses are actually attractive. There are some quite compact greenhouses however, and a few that have been designed to look pleasing as well as being useful. For the enthusiastic propagator, this will be an essential, but for those that are creating an aesthetic garden, it may well be a low priority. It really depends on your style of gardening and how important it is for you to have a greenhouse to grow plants.

Although greenhouses usually suggest hard work, the setting in this mature garden and addition of the deck chair suggest a quiet relaxing afternoon in the sun.

4 GREAT PLANTS FOR SMALL GARDENS

As gardeners nowadays we are spoilt for choice. There are so many wonderful plants available and from so many sources. Great gardens need good plants just as much as delicious food needs quality ingredients. This may sound obvious, but so often people have disappointing gardens full of mediocre plants and they can't understand why the results are not better. Someone will complain that a particular plant doesn't flower properly. When asked its name and where it was bought, the owner will rarely know the full name, and very often it's some giveaway orphan that's been struggling to stay alive for several years. Such unknowns are most unlikely ever to give good garden performance. Throw them out!

Choosing plants for a small garden is especially important as the space you have is limited, and every inhabitant of your garden must pay its way without spreading too far. Plants should be correct to the scale of the space you are using. Vast park and forest trees will soon become problems and swamp a small space. Despite this, often oaks, chestnuts and other totally inappropriate trees are seen in small gardens. Many native plants are also far too big or invasive for small gardens, but despite this they are often inadvisably recommended to attract wildlife.

Big spreading shrubs such as buddleja and forsythia are often seen swamping a small garden, giving a very limited display in comparison to the space they are consuming. So many plants nowadays have more compact versions which are tailored for the small garden. People who care for small gardens need to be constantly aware of the eventual size of a plant when choosing, and always reject over-vigorous plants.

In a small garden you also need to consider how much interest a plant will contribute to your garden. For example, some plants such as flag iris or oriental poppies flower for just a few brief days and for the rest of the year are quite tiresome and boring. By contrast plants such as *Euphorbia wulfenii* will go on with their flowering display for many weeks and then the basic plant itself is evergreen, architectural and interesting even when out of flower. Other plants have more than one season of display so for example *Cornus alba* 'Aurea' has golden summer foliage and red winter twigs. Most pyracanthas are evergreen, have white flowers in early summer and brilliant berries in the autumn. The small flowered clematis such as *C. alpina* or *C. tangutica* have fluffy seedheads as well as flowers. Any plant that has more than one season of display gives extra interest in a small garden.

Plants are not expensive in comparison to many other items of garden expenditure. Compared to paving, walls and garden furniture, they are relatively cheap. If cared for, they will last for many years and give much pleasure, so buy the real thing and don't fill your garden with cast-offs and mongrels! Buy plants with proper names. Anything just labelled as mixed hybrids will probably be exactly as it says, a mixed bag, often grown from seed and mostly mediocre. Good gardening books and magazines will give many recommendations of good named plants, and you will see them performing in gardens open to the public and at flower shows. Buying plants in full

OPPOSITE: **A good planting scheme will include woody plants such as trees and shrubs as well as herbaceous perennials, and architectural plants such as the conifers and spiky phormiums in this garden.**

Modern gardens often use ornamental grasses which are associated here with colourful herbaceous perennials including the classic red *Dahlia* **'Bishop of Llandaff'.**

bloom at a garden centre is some indication of the potential performance of a plant – certainly not its full possibilities but a better indication than a coloured label.

One particular thing to look out for is the simple designation AGM, sometimes a cup symbol, after the name of a plant. This means Award of Garden Merit and is given by the Royal Horticultural Society for plants that have performed well in their trials. Such plants will have consistently achieved well in a garden situation, are of good constitution, resist pests and diseases and are generally available.

Good plants have many different characteristics, some more obvious than others. You might make an immediate choice of a plant because it catches your attention; maybe it's a favourite colour or fits a current craze you've got, for spiky plants or foliage or whatever. Your choices are all very personal. But there will be other less obvious

characteristics. The length of display has already been mentioned. Also consider hardiness. Promoters of garden plants can sometimes be rather liberal in their interpretation of winter hardiness. Do check out whether a plant is likely to survive over winter in your area without protection. Other characteristics will affect the end result in more complex ways. For example many modern plants will have disease-resistance bred in to them. Many old fashioned roses may have quite beautiful flowers but are prone to diseases such as mildew and black spot. Unless you want heritage cultivars and are willing to spend a lot of time spraying, it would be better to avoid them and choose good modern ones. Some plants have a weak constitution and may not last many years. This is where looking for recommendations such as the AGM gives assurance of a plant that will perform well in the garden, not just look good in the garden centre.

SKELETON PLANTING

A good garden will have a strong 'bone structure' which includes not only the hard landscape elements such as paving, walls, fences, arbours and features but also the permanent planting. Permanent woody planting such as trees, shrubs and climbers give the garden a sense of permanence and maturity at any season and will always be key components of any design. This is sometimes called skeleton planting.

Trees

Trees are important elements of any garden, and every garden – however small – should have at least one good, carefully chosen tree. They give height, maturity, often act as highlights and may have a whole host of other features such as flowers, foliage, berries or interesting bark. Although many trees may be far too big for a small garden, there are numerous species which are slow growing, compact and have upright habits which make them suitable for a small space. Those which are narrow, with either a pyramidal or fastigiate habit, are ideal for a small garden as they do not take up much floorspace and won't cast too much shade. For example *Pyrus calleryana* 'Chanticleer' is an ornamental pear that grows slowly to a height of 6m (20ft). It has a lovely narrow tailored shape and produces clouds of white pear blossom in early spring. Throughout the summer it is covered by glossy dark green foliage which becomes rich orange and then red before it drops in the autumn.

Trees are usually sold by size, which is a measurement of their stem diameter. A 12–14cm tree will be a good-sized standard tree, around 3–4m (10–13ft) tall with instant impact. Always make sure the roots are moist and preferably rootballed, which means wrapped in a ball of soil and sacking or polythene. Container grown trees are essential for summer planting and will be more expensive. An 8–10cm tree, about 2.75m (9ft) tall, will be in a 45 litre container of compost which is a heavy item to transport. A few trees such as birch and amelanchier may also be available as multi-stem

Acer pseudoplatanus 'Brilliantissimum' is a welcome relative of sycamore, making a compact, mop-headed tree with dazzling spring and early summer foliage.

trees, and will probably have two to four stems arising from ground level. A group of gnarled white birch stems set amongst a green lawn can look quite spectacular.

Trees are long-term features in a garden and need to be located carefully. Once established they will be dominant amongst your planting and may well be one of the strongest features in the whole garden. Remember also that in time trees will tend to impoverish the soil and cast shade. Their value in contributing to privacy has already been mentioned. Also avoid planting a tree close to drains, water or gas pipes and cables.

TREES FOR SMALL GARDENS

Tree	Description	Height
Pyrus salicifolia 'Pendula' AGM	Small weeping tree with silvery grey foliage	4m (13ft)
Betula pendula 'Youngii'	Weeping silver birch, a perfect umbrella shape	3m (10ft)
Betula pendula 'Golden Beauty' AGM	Elegant golden foliage	4m (13ft)
Prunus 'Amanogawa'	Upright, very narrow, sugar pink cherry blossom	5m (16ft)
Acer negundo 'Flamingo'	Pink and white variegated foliage	3.6m (12ft)
Gleditsia triacanthos 'Sunburst' AGM	Delicate golden foliage	5m (16ft)
Acer pseudoplatanus 'Brilliantissimum' AGM	Mop headed, young leaves pink	3.6m (12ft)
Malus 'Golden Hornet' AGM	Upright, white flowers and yellow crabapples	5m (16ft)
Sorbus cashmiriana AGM	Upright, autumn colour, pink flowers and berries	5m (16ft)

Shrubs

Together with trees, shrubs are usually the most important plants in any garden. In using them you can create the skeleton of your garden on which all the other items of interest and colour are added. Shrubs are permanent plants, many of which are evergreen and have year-round interest in any planting scheme. They can provide shelter, a background winter structure and a whole host of other interesting features. Shrubs are the stalwarts of any garden. They can be used on their own, and indeed gardens with nothing but shrubs can be quite remarkable, but the finest gardens are those where shrubs are integrated with roses, herbaceous perennials, bulbs and seasonal bedding plants. Such planting schemes fairly sizzle with colour and appeal.

This beautiful blue flowered *Hydrangea* 'Zorro' is an ideal companion for the fiery foliage of *Berberis* 'Orange Rocket', both fairly new introductions.

This small garden has an excellent arrangement of trees, shrubs, evergreens and architectural plants which will give it structure and interest at all seasons.

Evergreen shrubs are important because they give interest during the winter months when a garden can otherwise be quite drab and lifeless. Choose evergreens carefully and avoid having too many with coloured leaves. Whilst plants such as *Elaeagnus pungens* 'Maculata' can be quite spectacular and provide a touch of winter sunshine, a garden with too many white, gold or spotted leaf shrubs can appear strident. By all means include variegated plants, but site them carefully and use sparingly. Green leaves need not be boring. They come in all sorts of sizes, different shades of green, a multitude of leaf shapes, some with smooth edges and others with jagged or curly boundaries. The interplay between different leaves gives a complex mix of textures amongst plants. Many evergreens will also give you interesting flowers

such as *Choisya* 'Aztec Pearl' which has white sweetly scented flowers in early summer.

Amongst the flowering shrubs, there is an enormous range to choose from. Once again, look for species and cultivars that are relatively compact and have a fairly long season of display, and check for dwarf versions of old favourites. Decide if you want your garden to peak at one particular season or if you wish to ensure that there is interest throughout the year. Although there are probably more shrubs that have their main display in early summer than at any time, there are species which will flower during any month of the year including the depths of winter. Many deciduous shrubs also have variegated or coloured foliage, sometimes as well as flowers. They will have a long season of interest, but like evergreens, use sparingly to avoid a garish effect.

Try to include as many plants as possible which have a second display feature. Scent has already been mentioned, which is a bonus from the flowering shrubs. As well as scented flowers, some shrubs have aromatic foliage, such as lavender and the wonderful lemon scented *Aloysia citriodora*. Some such as cotoneaster and pyracantha will also produce autumn berries; in fact the berries on both of those are certainly more attractive than the flowers. For winter interest, you may wish to grow shrubs with interesting stems, particularly members of the genus *Cornus* – the dogwoods. *Cornus alba* 'Aurea' has lovely golden leaves in the summer, and when these drop in the autumn sealing wax red stems are revealed which provide valuable winter colour. If left untouched, the dogwoods can become rather too big, but they respond well to hard pruning in late spring, which results in vigorous stems, lush foliage and good stem colour the next winter, all on a compact plant. Some plants, such as the globe artichoke, runner beans, some salads and many herbs, can be ornamental as well as providing edible fruit or vegetables. Definitely good value!

Hedges

Hedges are basically rows of shrubs that are usually clipped to create a formal barrier or wall of green. Historically yew and box have been widely used in many wonderful gardens, but as well as these, hedges have a bad name as many people will immediately think of the ubiquitous privet.

Depending on what you choose, hedges can also give a display of flowers or berries. A pyracantha hedge will be evergreen, with dark green leaves all the year, white flowers in early summer and a display of colourful berries in autumn and early winter. Be sure to prune flowering hedges at the right season so you do not inadvertently leave them without blooms and destroy the display.

Hedges do not have to be all of the same species. For example, the pyracantha hedge mentioned might be made up of two or three different cultivars, giving berries in different colours. If you plant a beech hedge it can be very effective to use about ten per cent of plants of copper beech. Space them irregularly, and they will grow through the hedge in a random pattern, giving interesting splashes of purple foliage.

DOUBLE DISPLAY SHRUBS

Shrub	Description	Height
Pyracantha 'Saphyr Orange' AGM	Evergreen, white flowers and orange berries	1.8m (6ft)
Perovskia 'Blue Spire' AGM	Silvery aromatic foliage and blue flowers	90cm (3ft)
Sarcococca hookeriana AGM	Evergreen, pink winter flowers, scent, black berries	60cm (2ft)
Cornus alba 'Ivory Halo'	Silvery variegated foliage and red winter stems	1.2m (4ft)
Choisya ternata 'Sundance' AGM	Evergreen, golden foliage and scented white flowers	90cm (3ft)
Hamamelis x intermedia 'Diane' AGM	Fragrant ruby flowers in winter, autumn colour	1.5m (5ft)
Lavandula 'Grosso'	Aromatic silver foliage and blue flowers	45cm (18in)
Cotoneaster horizontalis 'Variegata'	Variegated foliage, white flowers and red berries	60cm (2ft)

Climbers and Wall Shrubs

These plants are particularly useful in a small garden, as quite a few can usually be squeezed in without taking up a great deal of extra space. Somebody once said that 'you own the space above your garden as far as you can use it'. Whether that is technically correct is neither here nor there, but it can nevertheless be useful to go up when you can't spread out. So therefore make sure you use the walls of your house, your fences and any other opportunity to grow climbing plants.

There are species suitable for almost any situation from full sun through to dense shade. Maybe you have a hot dry south facing wall, so you might choose to grow an abutilon such as 'Kentish Belle', which will revel in the warmth and produce a succession of orange yellow, bell shaped flowers throughout the summer. Then a cold north facing wall would be ideal for *Hydrangea petiolaris*, the climbing hydrangea or one of the many variegated ivies such as *Hedera colchica* 'Sulphur Heart' with its huge green leaves splashed with vivid yellow.

Climbers come in several categories, according to how they grow. All the ivies and the climbing hydrangea produce aerial roots that cling to rough surfaces like stonework. These can be planted against a wall and left to grow on their own without any support. Unless the mortar between the bricks is actually loose and crumbling, they will not harm the building. However, you will need to be careful if they grow vigorously and reach the roof line, as they are inclined to creep under the tiles and invade your roof space.

Some climbers such as the ornamental vine *Vitis coignetiae* have waving tendrils that will grab hold of anything nearby. Virginia creeper is similar but with suckers on the end of its tendrils which help it to stick. Clematis leaves have long flexible stalks which can curl around twigs or small supports. The summer jasmine, *Jasminum officinale*, has twining stems which wind around a support or other plants. The golden leaved culti-

This modern formal garden makes full use of hedges with beautiful examples of close-clipped box, yew and beech hedging.

var 'Fiona Sunrise' is particularly attractive with fragrant white flowers as well as buttercup yellow foliage. All of these are ideal for growing on trellises, up pergolas and obelisks. If you want these on a fence or brick or concrete walls you will need to provide a supporting trellis or alternatively a matrix of galvanized wires fixed to the wall. Wires are a very useful way of supporting climbers; inconspicuous when first installed and rapidly disappearing as the climbers grow.

As well as true climbers, there are a whole host of plants correctly known as wall shrubs, which are usually grown against a wall or fence. They include plants like abutilon, which are very lax in their habit of growth and will benefit from being trained against a support. Others are slightly

TOP: **This sunny coloured hardy ivy, correctly known as** *Hedera colchica* **'Sulphur Heart' but sometimes sold as 'Paddy's Pride', is ideal for a shady north wall.**

BELOW: **Many climbers will grow successfully together, like this** *Clematis* **'Perle d'Azur' happily co-habiting with the climbing 'Iceberg' rose.**

CLIMBERS

For Sunny Walls	Description	Height
Clematis montana 'Tetrarose' AGM	Large satin pink flowers over ruby tinted foliage	5m (15ft)
Wisteria sinensis AGM	Vigorous climber with scented blue trailing flowers in early summer	8m (25ft)
Fremontodendron californicum 'California Glory' AGM	Brilliant golden yellow saucer shaped flowers in mid summer	3m (10ft)
Campsis x tagliabuana 'Madame Galen' AGM	Clusters of tomato red trumpets in mid to late summer	3m (10ft)

For Shady Walls		
Garrya elliptica 'James Roof' AGM	Dark green leaves with long silvery catkins all winter	3m (10ft)
Jasminum nudiflorum AGM	Small yellow flowers produced on green stems all winter	3m (10ft)
Hydrangea petiolaris AGM	White lacecap flowers in mid summer, self-clinging	3m (10ft)
Hedera colchica 'Sulphur Heart' AGM	Large glossy green leaves with bold splash of pure sunshine yellow	3m (10ft)

For Obelisks and Trellises		
Clematis viticella 'Etoile Violette' AGM	Purple flowers with creamy yellow centre	2.1m (7ft)
Rosa 'Gertrude Jekyll' AGM	Glowing pink roses with rich scent	1.8m (6ft)
Lonicera periclymenum 'Belgica'	Rosy purple flowers with yellow lips and rich honeysuckle fragrance in early summer	1.8m (6ft)
Jasminum officinale 'Fiona Sunrise'	Delicate golden yellow foliage with bonus of scented white flowers in mid summer	3m (10ft)

tender such as *Cytisus battandierii* and will benefit from the protection of a south or west facing wall.

Do remember that you can also grow many climbers up established trees. Let's say you have a much loved apple tree in your garden. You might want to add to it a climbing rose such as 'Wedding Day' which will scramble through the tree almost unseen and then pop out all over the crown with masses of small, cream, sweetly scented flowers. You can also install at the base of the same tree a plant of the golden leaved ivy 'Jester's Gold' which will cover the lower trunk with a coat of pointed golden leaves. Think through the flowering seasons of mixed planting – don't make the mistake of planting *Clematis montana* in apple trees, for example, as both flower at the same time with very pale pink flowers and the effect is rather lost. If the growth of your chosen climbers seems too slow for you, do consider annual climbers such as *Cobaea scandens*, *Rhodochiton atrosanguineus*, *Eccremocarpus scaber* or *Ipomoea lobata*, which will all provide some quick temporary cover and colour while your permanent residents mature.

Conifers

These are a distinct group of plants, now rather unfashionable. The overuse of forest conifers such as Leyland cypress in small gardens has totally blackened their name. However some of the slow growing species, such as *Pinus mugo* and ground-cover types of juniper, are excellent evergreens with strong shapes, many having coloured foliage in green, gold and blue/grey. If choosing an upright conifer for an accent, choose carefully. *Chaemaecyparis lawsoniana* 'Pembury Blue' has a good narrow habit, bluish grey foliage and is not too vigorous. Remember that conifers can be lightly trimmed to keep in shape but never hard pruned.

Roses

Roses are often seen as traditional English garden plants, and many gardeners will want to include a few for their colour and scent. There are thousands of cultivars of roses available, some of which are good and most of which are quite ordinary or even mundane. Most traditional bush roses are really too rigid for the style of modern gardens. Formal rose beds just do not fit into contemporary gardens, and standard roses are decidedly horrid. Although many shrub roses are lovely, avoid the older types such as 'Canary Bird' or 'Nevada' which make huge bushes but flower only once briefly each summer.

Ground cover and patio roses can be very suitable for a small garden, as many of them make quite compact plants and are perpetual flowering. The 'County Series' has a wide colour range, and the compact bushes can be covered with small rose blooms for much of the summer.

If you want taller plants and scent, check out the roses bred by David Austin. Over a number of years, this rose breeder has produced a number of cultivars which have all the charm of traditional English roses, complete with perfume but without many of the bad traits of older cultivars. These roses are compact, with a long season of flower and generally disease-resistant. One of the most successful is 'Graham Thomas', a lovely rich golden yellow double with a strong perfume and good disease resistance. 'Gertrude Jekyll' is a warm glowing pink. Climbing roses can be useful in small gardens as they can be trained back to trellises or tripods.

COSMETIC PLANTING

Whereas the skeleton planting – trees and shrubs – give the 'bones' of your garden, cosmetic planting adds the softer elements that give 'flesh' to the structure you have created. For this you can use the whole host of colourful herbaceous perennials, grasses, bulbs and bedding plants available. These are more than just fillers, so they should always be an integral part of the basic design, adding the final detail and interest that will complete a good planting scheme. Sometimes gardeners ignore the importance of the skeleton planting and concentrate on cosmetic planting

'Graham Thomas' is one of the best of the New English roses bred by David Austin, combining fragrance and a traditional form with a strong constitution.

The rich foliage of *Heuchera* 'Blackberry Jam' tones perfectly with the flowers of *Campanula takesimana*, complemented by the silvery tints of *Athyrium niponicum* 'Pictum'.

only, and this gives a weak ineffective result. A good well-balanced scheme of skeleton and cosmetic planting will be colourful and dynamic throughout the summer, with the whole planting contributing to the effect. In the winter months when the perennials become dormant and bedding dies, the woody plants, and particularly the evergreens, will become more dominant, giving enough structure and providing a different kind of interest until spring.

Herbaceous Perennials

It is especially important with herbaceous perennials to buy good cultivars. Even though you are planting a small garden, try to plant perennials in groups of threes, fives or sevens. Such blocks of foliage and colour will be far more effective than individual plants. Amongst the many species available, *Alchemilla mollis*, *Geranium* 'Johnson's Blue', *Sedum spectabile* 'Brilliant', *Rudbeckia* 'Goldsturm' and *Coreopsis verticillata* 'Moonbeam' are particularly reliable.

In recent years a whole host of cultivars of heuchera have been bred. The most familiar of the these is 'Palace Purple' which makes a small bun shaped plant covered in rich purple, wavy leaves. It is evergreen, so looks good in the winter as well, and in early summer it has the added bonus of a haze of delicate white flowers on slender stalks. There are many other cultivars available such as 'Crème Brûlée' with soft apricot foliage, 'Key Lime Pie' with pale apple green leaves and some very dark cultivars such as 'Liquorice'. All are excellent ground cover plants in bright sun or light shade.

A few herbaceous perennials are big and bold enough to plant as specimens, and species such as *Crambe cordifolia*, *Cortaderia selloana* (pampas grass), *Macleaya cordata* and *Euphorbia wulfenii* 'Lambrook Gold' will all make big plants and solid statements. The euphorbias are a useful group of plants. They are semi-evergreen so their greyish green foliage looks good in the winter, and most produce striking heads of lime green bracts in early summer.

The bergenias are also valuable plants, usually listed with perennials, although they too are ever-green and do not die down in the winter. Many gardeners will know them as elephant's ears for their huge broad, glossy green leaves. With some such as 'Ballawley' and 'Evening Glow', the leaves turn a warm bronze in winter. Most flower in early spring in shades of pink, the darkest of which is 'Evening Glow' with ruby flowers and there is also 'Silver Light' with almost white flow-ers. They are wonderfully tolerant plants which will grow almost anywhere in sun or shade and provide a dark green mass of handsome foliage. Surprisingly many people seem to dislike them.

This colourful group of groundcover plants features the golden grassy foliage of *Carex elata* 'Aurea', sometimes called Bowle's golden sedge.

The dark foliage of *Geranium* 'Midnight' and *Ajuga* 'Braun Hertz' contrast well with the golden foliage of *Acorus gramineus* 'Ogon' and *Carex oschimensis* 'Evergold'.

They contrast well with epimediums, a creeping herbaceous perennial with delicate glossy leaves that is also semi-evergreen. These grow well in the shade and produce frail flowers in shades of yellow and red.

Ornamental Grasses

Ornamental grasses are another group within herbaceous perennials that make a valuable contribution to a planting scheme and are currently quite fashionable. Grasses have a distinct annual cycle, growing from a tufty crown to a full-blown bouquet of foliage, often topping this with a filigree of flowers by autumn. What's more, they move with the breeze and finally take on a beauty of their own when russet in winter and touched by a dusting of frost. Add to this the huge range of grasses and you have enormous potential.

Amongst the grasses, are a number of quite compact well-behaved types that are highly suitable for a small garden. *Miscanthus* 'Kleine Silberspinne' has green foliage and spidery red tinged flowers in late summer. It associates well with most other herbaceous perennials. *Stipa gigantea* makes a striking plant with waving heads of golden oat-like flowers growing to about 1.5m (5ft) tall. It's a good specimen plant.

At the other end of the scale we have *Hakonechloa macra* 'Aureola', a low-growing, groundcover grass growing to about 25cm (9in) with weeping ribbon-like foliage striped in green and gold. Look out for the lovely new pure yellow version called 'All Gold'. The various different types of *Festuca glauca* are very tolerant and will put up with dry and shady locations. The species has dainty silvery foliage topped with delicate bluish green flowers. 'Elijah Blue' is an intense steely blue and 'Golden Toupee' has curious almost lime-green leaves. Although botanically a sedge, *Carex* 'Evergold' looks like an evergreen grass, making a small spiky bundle of yellow and green foliage that is just as bright in winter as in summer and will grow almost anywhere.

The deep blue agapanthus and the ruby red sedum act as perfect foils for the brilliant orange flowers of the taller *Lilium lancifolium* 'Flore Plena'.

Groundcover Plants

Many different types of plant, both shrubs and herbaceous, can be put in this category. A groundcover plant is anything which will grow strongly, make a dense canopy of foliage and therefore cover the soil, preventing the emergence of weeds. Most good groundcover plants are low growing and will often be used underneath other taller plants.

So for example, you might have some lovely deciduous azaleas, growing to about 1.2m (4ft). These could be underplanted with winter heathers. The azaleas flower in early summer,

have good autumn colour and then drop their leaves. Heathers are evergreen and flower in midwinter. A bed of old English roses could be under planted with *Geranium* 'Johnson's Blue', although this is not a perfect choice as the geranium being herbaceous will die down to the ground in the winter. Groundcover plants do not have to be short. Plants such as the dense growing *Choisya ternata* 'Sundance' will be effective at preventing the weed growth, even though its eventual height is likely to be nearly a metre.

Spring and Summer Bulbs

Bulbs are a very effective way of adding extra colour to a small garden, as they can be tucked in between existing plants, taking up very little space and giving lots of seasonal colour. The whole host of spring bulbs, including tulips, narcissus, hyacinths and all the tiny little bulbs such as crocus, iris, muscari and chionodoxa are generally well-known and readily available. They need to be planted in the autumn to provide colour the following spring.

Crocuses and narcissi are usually the earliest to flower and give us the first hint that spring is on its way. These can be sited in your borders in places where they can survive from year to year, becoming bigger clumps with more flowers as time goes on.

However tulips do not seem to survive quite so well and so it's probably best to consider them as 'one-hit wonders' and replant them each year. Bulbs are not expensive and the rewards from their explosions of colour well justify the cost. Tulips are also excellent plants in containers, but plant them generously. Decide how many you think your pot will take and double the number, nestling them in tightly when you plant. The resulting volume of colour will be well worth the extra bulbs. Mixing together two different

OPPOSITE: *Cosmos* 'Sonata Pink' is an annual bedding plant that provides additional zing to the permanent planting of phormium, cortaderia and *Crocosmia* 'Solfatare'.

cultivars of tulip can be very effective, but you need to be sure that they will flower at the same time. So for example the snowy white 'Shirley' looks good planted with the rich purple 'Attila', or the soft iridescent orange 'Jimmy' with the almost black 'Ronaldo'.

Summer bulbs are often forgotten, but just like their spring counterparts, they can be squeezed in amongst other plants. Probably lilies are the most useful, providing striking stately heads in a dazzling range of colours. *Lilium regale* is a good reliable white with a rich scent. There are numerous yellow cultivars such as 'Connecticut King', pinks such as the well-known 'Stargazer' and orange shades such as 'Enchantment'. The tall growing *Lilium lancifolium* 'Flore Plena' makes a handsome plant with vivid double orange flowers covered in black spots. Lilies should be planted in autumn or early spring, and if you put them direct in the ground, set them on a small bed of grit or sharp sand for extra drainage. Alternatively plant the bulbs individually in 12.5cm (5in) pots and then pop them into their permanent location when they are growing strongly. Having a few plants growing on like this can be very useful for filling gaps. Try to see gaps not as problems but as opportunities for creating something spontaneously.

Amongst the other summer bulbs, there is an enormous range of alliums – ornamental onions – usually in shades of pink or white, producing delicate globular flowers. Crocosmias are often sold as herbaceous perennials, but they do actually grow from small corms. 'Lucifer' is a good red, and 'Solfatare' is a glowing gold over lightly sunburned foliage. Gladioli are not fashionable and are rather stiff for most planting schemes, but they do provide intense colour. You either love them or hate them! Eucomis, the pineapple lilies are valuable for late summer colour, in particular the purple leaved form of *Eucomis comosa*. For late summer the hardy *Cyclamen hederifolium* is a charming species producing small white or pale pink flowers. Grow it in semi-shade for best results; the flowers are followed by dark green foliage with pretty white marblings in winter and early spring.

Bedding Plants

This group of colourful plants has been much maligned in recent years, but amongst the bedding plants we have a wonderful palette of fast growing plants that will give instant colour for six months of the year. Some bedding is grown from seed, although many modern cultivars are produced from cuttings. Plants grown from seed are not necessarily poor. Some plants breed true to type and will be predictable. Also those known as F1 hybrids are likely to give a good display because of very select plant breeding. F1 hybrids are always more expensive than non-hybrids, but the extra cost will be recouped in a far better display, longer flowering, greater pest and disease resistance and other characteristics. Many annuals and other seasonal display plants are also trialled in various locations all round Europe by an organization called Fleuroselect. A plant with a Fleuroselect award (a logo with two linked red flowers) is very likely to be a good plant. Use bedding plants in key locations and containers for maximum effect. Be selective and use single colours rather than mixtures, which can be tasteless, and blend the plants with coloured foliage.

Particularly useful plants include the various types of *Begonia* 'Non Stop', *Cosmos* 'Sonata White', dark-leaved dahlias, rudbeckias, tall antirrhinums, *Nicotiana sylvestris* (syn. 'Only the Lonely') and verbenas such as the 'Quartz' strains. For annual foliage, try Millet 'Purple Majesty', coloured-leaved pelargoniums and coleus.

PLANTS TO AVOID

There are certain plants to avoid in small gardens. Initially do not be tempted to plant any forest or parkland trees such as oak, ash, sycamore or horse chestnut. A small 'conker tree' will soon become a monster dominating your garden. Avoid invasive spreading bamboos such as *Sasa veitchii*, which will not only march relentlessly across your garden but make you consider moving house when you attempt to dig it out! Politely refuse offers of unnamed giveaways from neighbours. If they spread rapidly enough for your neighbour to have surplus, then they are probably too aggressive for a small space. Bargain shrubs in local supermarkets simply labelled as 'Forsythia', 'Weigelia' or 'Pyracantha' will not be good value. They are likely to be old unimproved cultivars, generally very vigorous and of limited garden value. Other plants such as *Iris germanica*, rhododendrons and oriental poppies look great for a couple of weeks each year but then look dreary or downright untidy for the other fifty weeks. Enjoy them in other people's gardens and avoid wasting precious space in yours. In general terms, the bigger the eventual size of a plant, the more you should consider whether its value is worth the precious space it will take in your special plot.

The cinnamon coloured irises in these containers look great, but their short flowering period make them a poor choice for such a key feature.

5 BEING CREATIVE WITH PLANTS

Putting plants together in the garden to create an exciting effect is just as creative as painting or drawing. However we are dealing with living plants which grow and change with time, and that makes it even more challenging. All plants have a number of characteristics, the most basic being colour, texture and form. Colour is self-explanatory but does of course encompass the colour of leaves, berries and stems as well as flowers, all of which alter with the seasons.

Texture and form need some explanation. Texture refers to the pattern that a plant's leaves, or flowers, make. This can be most quickly explained by comparing the tiny green leaves on a box plant with a huge waving leaves on a banana tree. The box produces a very delicate fine texture, which is very different to the broad smooth surfaces of the banana leaf. Fine textures have little difference between the surfaces that catch the light and the shadows behind, but with big leaves, the differences between light and shade are dramatic, which gives large leaved plants their punch. Some plants have leaves that may be large but have a fine texture, such as a tree fern whose leaves may be over a metre long but comprised of hundreds of tiny little leaflets.

Form, sometimes called structure, is all about the shape of a plant, which can be rounded, upright and narrow; low and spreading like a cushion; spiky or trailing. Plants with particularly striking shapes or outlines are often described as

OPPOSITE: **Successful planting schemes often evolve over a number of years, as different plants and combinations are tried and refined and as plants mature.**

architectural plants. They can be especially useful as specimens, set in key locations in a planting scheme or even positioned on their own as highlights in a lawn. *Viburnum tomentosum* 'Mariessii' is a good example. As it grows, it produces branches as tiered layers and when in full bloom, laden with white flowers in early summer, it can be quite spectacular. Other plants may have a spiky outline such as the many types of phormium (New Zealand flax) or the more compact yuccas. Bamboos will also come into this category, having a very dominant vertical shape, appealing canes and foliage. Others may be of particular interest because they have especially bold shiny foliage such as *Fatsia japonica*, the false castor oil plant, with big glossy green hand-shaped leaves.

Contrasting together different shapes is one way of adding interest to a planting scheme. The upright habit of a clump of black bamboo, *Phyllostachys nigra*, could be contrasted with a big spreading carpet of *Euonymus* 'Sunspot'. In some cases gardeners force a particular form onto a plant by the way it is pruned or trimmed. Both yew and box are available in a whole range of shapes from cubes and balls through to pyramids, cones or spirals. Such fancy shapes can provide exciting highlights in a planting scheme.

BORDERS NEEDN'T BE BORING

Beds and borders will come in all sorts of shapes and sizes. In a small garden, they can sometimes be too narrow to be really useful. Ideally for a good progression from front to back and to allow for contrasting heights and shapes, borders should be at least 1.8m (6ft) wide. In many situations this will not be so.

A border with a width of 90cm (3ft) or less will only really accommodate one row of shrubs with some perennials, so the opportunities immediately become limited. Many of the taller shrubs will be as wide as they are tall, so using anything with height will immediately mean that the planting juts out into the rest of the garden. In narrow borders, wall shrubs and climbers become very useful as you can have height and impact without too much encroachment. Occasionally you may have to contend with borders as narrow as 30cm (1ft). Climbers and a few low-growing groundcover plants are really the only options, but with the range of climbers available, even this need not be tedious.

Hitting the Heights

When designing a planting scheme, one of the most important things to remember is that you are working in several dimensions. It is sometimes difficult, when working on a sheet of paper, to imagine what plants will be like in reality and when they have reached their final stature.

Start off by marking in key plants such as trees and specimen shrubs that will act as the highlights and usually the tallest points within your border. Plants are usually simply drawn on a plan as scaled circles, roughly corresponding to their mature diameter. Depending on the size and shape, there may be any number of key plants, but often three, five or seven is useful. So for example you might include a small tree such as *Betula utilitis*, a lovely white stemmed birch, with an architectural evergreen such as *Fatsia japonica* and a spiky leaved plant such as *Phormium tenax* 'Atropurpureum'. These three would be positioned in a triangle, never in a row, in such a way as to mark the basic extent of the border. Specimen plants such as these are essential to emphasize the shape of the border and act like full stops. They may be individual plants or groups.

Establishing the Skeleton

At this stage, start to create a matrix of strongly structural plants throughout the area. It is likely that a high proportion of these should be evergreens, although good strong growing roses and deciduous shrubs can also be used. In choosing these plants be aware of the backgrounds you are creating for the specimens you have already positioned. So you might plant a group of the golden leaved *Choisya ternata* 'Sundance' around the dark leaved phormium. As well as providing a contrasting background, they will give you scented white flowers in early summer. At this

Evergreen *Phormium* 'Yellow Wave' and *P.* 'Atropurpurea' contrasted with the golden foliage of *Cornus alba* 'Aurea', some ornamental grasses and blue lavender.

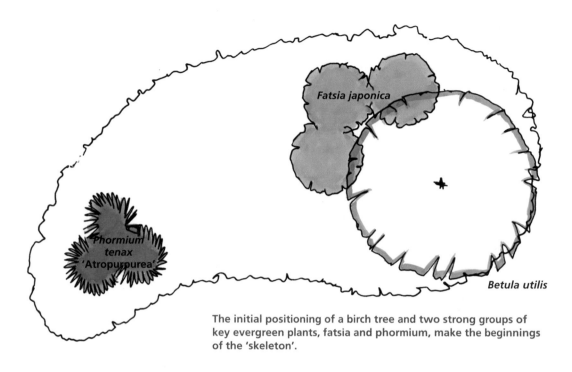

The initial positioning of a birch tree and two strong groups of key evergreen plants, fatsia and phormium, make the beginnings of the 'skeleton'.

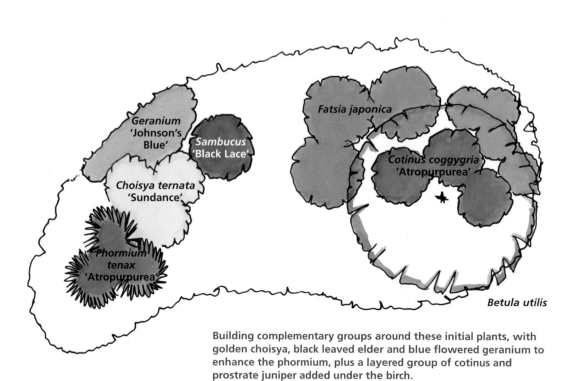

Building complementary groups around these initial plants, with golden choisya, black leaved elder and blue flowered geranium to enhance the phormium, plus a layered group of cotinus and prostrate juniper added under the birch.

The planting in this garden uses a wide colour range, but the generous addition of grasses, bamboos and green box edging makes this successful.

stage you have really created the skeleton of your border on which you can then build the detail with smaller shrubs, roses and herbaceous perennials. Contrary to traditional notions, tall plants do not always need to be positioned at the back of a border or the middle of an island bed. Plant some taller, well-shaped plants towards the front to give extra punch.

Good Associations

As you compose a planting scheme, you will always be trying to consider colour, texture and form as you put plants together to create stunning groups. Although a planting scheme for a border or even a whole garden may have an overall colour scheme and style, it is usually made up of a number of smaller components that are called plant associations. Putting together the black leaved *Sambucus* 'Black Lace' with the golden foliage of *Choisya* 'Sundance' and the blue flowers of *Geranium* 'Johnson's Blue' will give a lovely cameo group – three different heights, some contrasting colours and an interesting mix of textures. Continuing to fill out your border, don't just stick in individual plants that you like but use groups of plants that make good associations.

Repetition

Try also to use more than single specimens of all but the largest plants – threes, fives, sevens and so on seem to be most effective. In a large border it helps if you repeat some of the plants or groups at intervals down the border or garden. In the example the use of the blue geranium is repeated. This

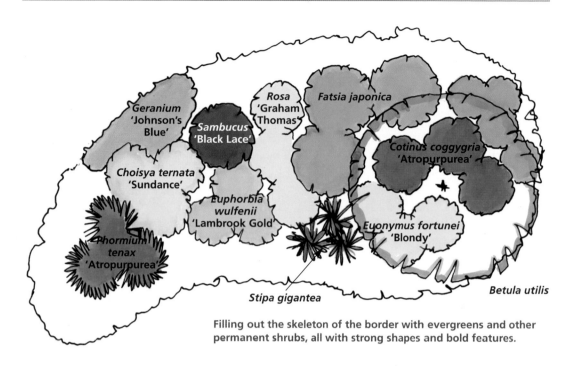

Filling out the skeleton of the border with evergreens and other permanent shrubs, all with strong shapes and bold features.

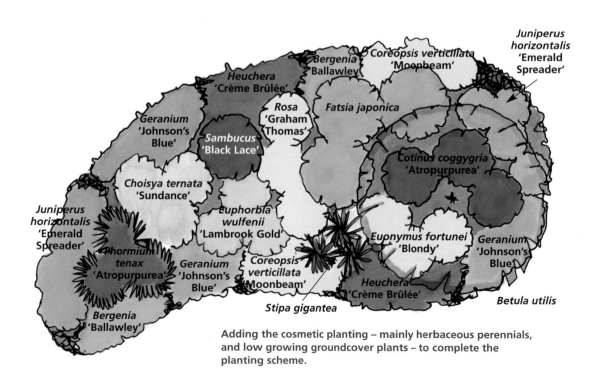

Adding the cosmetic planting – mainly herbaceous perennials, and low growing groundcover plants – to complete the planting scheme.

gives cohesion and is sometimes called rhythm. Although variety creates interest, many gardeners are tempted to use too many different plants, so repeating a favourite plant throughout the scheme gives a unifying element. Such attention to detail is the way to achieve a spectacular garden.

Layering is another valuable planting technique, in all gardens, but especially so when space is restricted. So underneath your birch tree, there might be a group of three or five *Cotinus coggygria* 'Atropurpurea', their purple foliage contrasting with the white bark. And to finish off, a carpet of the silvery prostrate *Juniperus horizontalis* 'Emerald Spreader'.

Don't be disappointed if it doesn't look perfect the first year. Good gardens are never finished, and there is always the opportunity to change

Unusual colour combinations can sometimes be very effective, such as this soft orange kniphofia with pink flowered *Echinacea purpurea* gently blended with the hazy *Panicum virgatum*.

things and improve on them, year by year. Make notes during the summer when plants are in bloom, so that changes can be made at the appropriate season. Probably the greatest proponent of continual observation and gradual change was Vita Sackville-West, who created the beautiful gardens at Sissinghurst Castle. These are famous for their wonderful plant associations and attention to detail. In the small studio in the tower, you can still see some of the Vita's notebooks, outlining the changes needed to be made in her garden year by year.

Colour Schemes

Although emphasis should be placed on good form and texture in a planting design, the use of colour is also very important. Most effective plantings have a palette of colours which is less than the full spectrum. Mixing all colours together tends to produce a riotous but rarely successful result. To suggest that all colours go together in a garden is nonsense. In truth, mixed colours do not clash quite as much as indoors – the blue of sky, green of foliage and brown of soil do tend to soften jangling colours – but the result is rarely good.

Colour schemes are another very individual expression of our personality. Some will love hot colours, the bright oranges, reds and yellows. Others will crave a cooler and more restful mix of blues, pastel shades and silver. Both are totally acceptable. Sometimes a whole garden might be designed in a single colour, such as the famous white garden at Sissinghurst, but it is more likely that you will choose a colour scheme for a border or a small part of your garden. Some colour schemes will use strongly contrasting colours such as orange and blue or yellow and purple; others will be gentler with complementary colours that are close to each other, such as blue and lavender or yellow and apricot. Most pastel shades – colours with less intensity such as pink, pale blue or cream – can be used together. Whatever the colours chosen for your scheme, you can freely use white which goes with anything, including silver and also bronze foliage.

This unusual garden uses a wide range of plant material and especially dark colours,
highlighted by some silver foliage and the rich maroon flowers of *Cosmos atrosanguinea.*

Beware of too much coloured or variegated foliage in a planting scheme, particularly with dominant plants such as specimens and trees. That golden leaved *Robinia* 'Frisia' may look pretty in a garden centre but it will probably shriek when mature and dominating your garden. Likewise dark colours such as rich bronze foliage, deep maroon and midnight blues can be very attractive in catalogues but disappointing in the garden, particularly in shade. However if you can position plants so that the sun shines through them, then the effect of ruby red foliage or dark chocolatey flowers can be quite dramatic.

Really there are no rules governing the composition of a good planting scheme. It all depends on innovation, an eye for good combinations, trial and error. The late Christopher Lloyd was once asked how he devised his wonderful colour schemes. He replied dismissively and somewhat mischievously, saying that he put 'any old colours together'. Possibly he did put all colours together in an experimental way, wondering what the results would be, but it is likely he had some idea of the outcome. When he found successful combinations, he went on to repeat them throughout the garden.

PLANTING FASHIONS

There are many different ways of effectively arranging plants, and these have changed over the years. The general one described above which uses a mix of shrubs, roses, herbaceous perennials, bulbs and seasonal plants often produces the most spectacular results. It is correctly known as a mixed border, but the use of a wide palette of plants necessitates a complex maintenance regime. Cottage gardens are often based on the mixed border style, often aiming to use older heritage cultivars.

Back in the early twentieth century, many gardens included a herbaceous border, relying solely on herbaceous perennials, which although spectacular in mid summer, had little or no interest outside of that time. In later years this developed into the island border, which still concentrated on herbaceous perennials but could be viewed from all sides. These days mixed plantings with just a proportion of perennials have now really superseded these styles.

Prairie Border

One of the most popular approaches in recent years has been the prairie border, which aims to mimic the vast natural meadows of North America with herbaceous perennials and ornamental grasses. The garden version is inevitably a little contrived but aims to look natural and informal. Although you can plan some interest in the earlier months of the year, these borders often peak in late summer when the grasses are fully grown. There should be no attempt to plant in groups but the plants should be mixed freely as might have happened naturally. The effect should be a contrast between bold blocks of colour and a delicate haze provided by the flowering grasses and species such as the ethereal *Verbena bonariensis*. Prairie planting should ideally be planned so you can walk through the planting rather than experiencing it from a distance.

PLANTS FOR A PRAIRIE BED

Plant	Details	Height
Miscanthus sinensis 'Kleine Fontane' AGM	Grass with delicate upright foliage and delicate pinkish flowers	1.5m (5ft)
Panicum virgatum	Steely blue foliage topped with a froth of delicate grass flowers	1.5m (5ft)
Deschamsia cespitosa	Green grass foliage and clouds of delicate flowers	1.2m (4ft)
Helictotrichon sempervirens AGM	Bluish foliage and tall heads of oat-like flowers	90cm (3ft)
Cortaderia selloana 'Pumila' AGM	Dwarf pampas grass, making a bold mound of foliage, topped with huge flowerheads	1.5m (5ft)
Echinacea purpurea	Late summer perennial with big purple daisy flowers	1.2m (4ft)
Helenium 'Moerheim Beauty' AGM	Rusty orange flowers with prominent black centre	90cm (36in)
Rudbeckia fulgida 'Goldsturm' AGM	Perennial with big yellow daisies with black centres	60cm (2ft)
Verbena bonariensis AGM	Tall slender perennial with small mauve flowers, making a delicate filigree effect	1.2m (4ft)
Aster x frikartii 'Mönch' AGM	Compact Michaelmas daisy with blue flowers	75cm (2ft 6in)

Gravel gardens are also popular and often use many prairie species. They are frequently planted on dry sites using species tolerant of low moisture. Plants will often be planted through a horticultural membrane and then the whole site surfaced with gravel. The gravel and membrane retain moisture and reduce weed growth. Plants will however usually be allowed to spread and seed naturally.

And So to Bed

There may be occasions when a single species bed will provide the right emphasis for an effect you are creating. In the past roses were used to provide formal beds of colour and also seasonal bedding plants. Now it is more likely that you will want a more contemporary effect, possibly using a bed of grasses or foliage groundcover plants. Modern minimalist gardens are likely to be designed with a very small palette of plants, using them in large, stark blocks or drifts, contrasted with a few strongly shaped architectural plants.

Formal bedding has become unfashionable and certainly there is little place for badly designed mixes of clashing colours in a modern garden. However the huge palette of both summer and spring bedding plants should not be ignored. There are many modern innovative ways they can be used to provide focal points in a planting scheme.

The exotic style has attracted many devotees in recent years. Using a mix of both hardy and tender plants, there is an attempt to produce a lush jungle-like planting. Plants such as bananas, cannas, bamboos, and other exotic foliage will jostle with the voluptuous flowers of angel's trumpets and dahlias in a bold and colourful mix. Beware, however: it is a very labour intensive style of planting.

For low maintenance, a mix of shrubs and groundcover plants can still be very effective, providing due attention is given to a selection of plants with contrasting textures and shapes and with interest at various seasons. Avoid those such as a buddleja, lavender, caryopteris and so on that need annual pruning.

Most prairie plantings are at their peak in late summer, with daisy flowered species such as *Rudbeckia fulgida* 'Goldsturm' and *Echinacea purpurea* mingling with waving grasses.

CHOOSE PLANTS THAT WILL THRIVE, NOT SULK

This section is so important it really should be at the beginning of this chapter, so if you've read this far, don't skip this bit!

Select your plants carefully for the garden you have, and don't try to fight against the conditions. At the survey stage, you will have made an assessment of the soil type and also made a note of which parts are sunny and those that are shady. Amongst the huge range of plants available in nurseries and garden centres, there are species for almost any combination of conditions you can imagine, so select them and match them up carefully. If you have a shady border, choose shade loving plants and they will thrive and give you much pleasure. But if you insist on planting sun lovers there they will sulk and generally fail and be a constant disappointment.

There are several books that concentrate on plants for different locations and the internet is

This beautiful *Rhododendron roseum* 'Elegans' will need an acid soil to thrive, but it is also happy in partial shade, like the variegated dogwood and iris growing with it.

an amazing source of information. Whatever the combination, whether it be dry and shady, hot and sunny, or moist and cool, there are plants available that will thrive in just that spot, if you search them out.

With soil conditions, you can make some modifications, and so a badly drained soil can be improved by careful cultivation and the inclusion of compost and grit. If you are determined to grow rhododendrons and camellias – which like an acid soil, but yours is alkaline – adding large quantities of peat and treating the soil with flowers of sulphur will acidify it over a period of time, but it is a slow process. You would be better to grow a few plants in pots of acid compost. Sometimes your soil limitations will open up the possibility to grow plants that you had perhaps not considered. A damp spot in the shade would be ideal for many ferns, which will not tolerate sun or drying out.

WHERE TO BUY YOUR PLANTS

Shopping for plants for a new garden can be great fun, but also very expensive! Gardening is an ongoing process (maybe an addiction?) and many gardeners will want to continue expanding their collection of plants and trying new species. This means there is inevitably a real element of impulse shopping.

There are a variety of different places where you can source exciting plants. Many of the plants described in this book can be obtained at garden centres, local nurseries or DIY stores. In particular if you want large specimens of these, do shop around and you may even be able to do a deal with a local grower if you are buying enough. If you are planting a whole new garden, send the list of plants you want to two or three local suppliers for a competitive quotation.

The specialist nurseries are probably some of the most exciting places to buy plants. Throughout the UK there are hundreds of small nurseries, specializing in all sorts of unusual plants. Many specialist nurseries also attend rare plant fairs, which are held throughout the spring and summer. These are well worth visiting, as you may well discover unusual plants in small quantities, not available elsewhere. There is also the added bonus of advice from the nurseryman who has grown them.

The internet is also a valuable source of plants, as some small growers do not open to the public and only sell via mail-order. It is also well worth checking eBay for unusual plants and seeds, particularly in the spring and early summer months, and all sorts of plants are often available. The *RHS Plant Finder*, published each year, is available as a printed book or free online as a searchable database, providing information on nurseries and where to buy plants.

Plant Sizes

Plants can be purchased in different sizes, but inevitably the larger specimen sizes will cost considerably more. Plants are usually sold by the size of the container they are growing in, measured in litres. Occasionally the overall height may be mentioned, but beware: this may include the depth of the pot. It is worth buying the larger sized trees (see page 57) and also larger sizes – maybe 10 litres – for your key specimen shrubs. For most of your planting, 2 or 3 litre plants will be quite adequate, and for herbaceous perennials 1 litre plants are fine. In general it is better to use a greater quantity of smaller plants spaced slightly closer. They will usually establish more quickly than older specimens.

During the winter, some plants, particularly trees, roses and fruit bushes are available as open ground or bare root plants. This means they will have been dug up from a field and have exposed roots. These can be good value and will establish well, providing the roots have not dried out. Check bare root plants before buying and reject any that look dry.

STRETCHING THE SEASONS

Most gardeners will want the gardens around their house to look good for as long a period as possible, and so in choosing plants you should plan for succession, to ring the changes throughout the year. This does mean that there will not be any one spectacular show time but rather an ever-changing progression of different growth patterns and displays. You can plan for the colour emphasis of a garden to change with the seasons. For example, you might choose shrubs, bulbs and early perennials all in soft pastel shades for a spring display. This could be followed by summer plantings, all of which are in bold hot colours.

Gardens that change over the seasons will also be far more stimulating than those that look the same all year. So a garden that is full of the lush exuberance of perennials in midsummer will look totally different in autumn and winter when they will be cut back and tidied up. This is when you will see how important it is to have garden shapes and other features such as berries and autumn colour.

When purchasing plants, look for good healthy growth and vigorous plants that are well maintained and have not been sitting unsold for too long.

Although evergreens are undoubtedly useful for winter colour, they do tend to look the same throughout the year which means that the parts of the garden that rely heavily on evergreens do not change at any season. For this reason, using evergreens is not the primary way of providing winter colour, but don't dismiss them out of hand. A neat little parterre of clipped box hedging filled with flowering perennials will look wonderful in summer, and you will naturally focus on the colourful display. However in the winter months, when the perennials have died back, the clear geometric shapes of the green box hedging will become dominant once again and contribute to the winter landscape (see page 133).

There are many good plants that flower during the winter months. *Mahonia x media* 'Charity' is an upright evergreen with attractive spiky foliage that can be very useful amongst your skeleton planting in any border and will not clash with any summer colour scheme. Throughout most of the winter, however, it will thrill you with long racemes of lemon yellow flowers with a wonderful fragrance. There are many other delightful shrubs that flower in the depths of winter and really require very little specialist attention. Do however site winter blossoms out of the reach of early morning sunshine, as should such winter blossoms become frosted, they are more likely to survive if they thaw out slowly in the shade. So that means that most winter flowering species, including favourites such as camellia, are actually ideal for borders against north facing walls which are often thought to be difficult.

There are also a few winter flowering herbaceous perennials, such as the well-known hellebores and also *Iris unguicularis*. This species comes from warm Mediterranean areas, so plant it tight against a south or west facing brick wall where it will be baked in summer. During the winter it will reward you with a display of exquisitely marked powder blue flowers with a delicate scent. Don't forget that there are also many small bulbs that flower very early such as *Iris reticulata*,

This little garden under the shade of a birch copse looks pretty in its summer greenery, but no doubt also looks good in spring with bulbs and flowers from the mahonias and euphorbias.

WINTER FLOWERING SPECIES

Plant	Details	Height
Chimonanthus praecox	Deciduous shrub, sweetly scented yellow flowers	1.5m (5ft)
Skimmia japonica 'Rubella' AGM	Evergreen, red buds opening to white flowers	90cm (3ft)
Jasminum nudiflorum AGM	Straggly climber, yellow flowers produced on green stems all winter	3m (10ft)
Mahonia 'Charity' AGM	Evergreen, yellow flowers, fragrant	1.8m (6ft)
Viburnum x bodnantense 'Dawn' AGM	Deciduous shrub, pink flowers	1.5m (5ft)
Hamamelis x intermedia 'Pallida' AGM	Deciduous shrub, yellow flowers, autumn colour	1.8m (6ft)
Daphne mezereum	Deciduous shrub, pink flowers, poisonous	90cm (3ft)
Erica carnea	Evergreen, many cultivars, pink and white, spreading	30cm (1ft)
Garrya elliptica 'James Roof' AGM	Evergreen wall shrub, silver tassels in winter	3m (10ft)
Helleborus orientalis	Lenten rose, herbaceous, shades white, pink and purple	30cm (12in)
Iris unguicularis AGM	Herbaceous perennial, spiky foliage, blue flowers	45cm (18in)

Anemone blanda, Scilla siberica, Chionodoxa luciliae and the well-known crocus and snowdrops.

Keeping a garden looking attractive and interesting throughout twelve months in a temperate climate is quite a challenge but distinctly possible. To a certain extent it's relatively easy to have a garden looking good in the summer months, but to have interest during the winter you must plan carefully from an early stage. Gardens based on good clear shapes with strong features and which utilize a variety of materials as well as good planting are most likely to be attractive throughout the year.

Mahonia x media 'Charity' is an excellent architectural evergreen with bold foliage, a strong shape and the bonus of sweetly scented flowers throughout the winter months.

6 SOME INSPIRING SMALL GARDENS

So far you have dreamt about your perfect garden and then had to come down to earth by considering some of the realities and mundane essentials. You've read about the important aspects of garden design: creating spaces and shapes, formality and informality and choosing a style. You've explored the various garden materials such as paving, lawns, walls, arbours and features including water. In particular you've realized the characteristics and limitations of all the many plants you can use. Creating a great garden involves putting all this together in such a way that the garden works for the purpose you want and evolves into a growing piece of living art. As the design develops, you will find that you are automatically using some of the devices and tricks mentioned. You can then further refine your design by adding in other details to lift the garden to a greater level.

The designs illustrated here will demonstrate many of the principles already outlined, so you will find the twisted axis in the low maintenance scheme and the family garden, false perspective in the aromatic garden and the use of different levels in the Mediterranean garden. The wildlife garden is clearly informal, whereas the minimalist garden is very formal and geometric. All the schemes show a sense of balance, although the aromatic garden is the only (almost) symmetrical one.

The actual designs in this chapter could be rescaled and used for a real garden, but I hope that you will feel so inspired that you will want to design your own garden. The examples will however show you how different sized and shaped plots can be turned into very different gardens, fulfilling the dreams and needs of their owners. The list of styles and themes is not exhaustive; read another design book and you will undoubtedly come across others. Even more exciting, create your own style. Inspiration for gardens can come from all sorts of places – maybe a theme from something you've seen on holiday, a film or picture, or a person. So for example you may have visited and exhibition of expressionist art and come away with your mind full of bold shapes and swirling colours – use the idea!

The plant lists give a selection of plants that would be effective in each garden, but they are not exclusive nor are they meant to be complete planting schedules. Other similar plants can be added according to your taste and the size of the garden you are planting. Most of the plans were drawn for a small garden of about 8m × 11m, the sort of plot that might be found behind many small modern houses. The colours on the plans are representative and merely intended to help identify different areas and elements.

You may feel that some of these designs are a little contrived and possibly too complex for the average garden plot. Maybe this is so, but they aim to show how much can be included in a small garden, and that with thought and ingenuity spectacular gardens can be created in small spaces. Most of the designs can be easily simplified.

The pictures that accompany these designs are regrettably not of the same gardens in their finished state but of other gardens embracing similar themes and demonstrating the principles used.

OPPOSITE: **This delightful garden has a seaside theme with shingle, a timber 'pier' and a garden shed, which has been painted a fresh blue suggesting a beach chalet.**

THE PLANTER'S GARDEN

The owner of this garden is a 'plantaholic', so it is unashamedly a place for plants. It is designed to provide a variety of habitats to show off treasured plants to their maximum potential. This formal design is based on a series of overlapping circles, treated in different ways. The broad terrace incorporates an arid bed in one corner, just right for South African agapanthus, leaving plenty of space for potted plants. To one side a small bed is filled each summer with tender exotics, and above this towers a stooled foxglove tree, grown for its huge leaves. A low lavender hedge frames the view onto the main lawn. To the side, a block paved path follows the lawn, giving easy access to the many plants in the adjacent border. If the owner is tempted to rest, a seat set in a small formal arbour faces across the lawn to a specimen paper bark maple set amongst a border of winter flowering species.

RECOMMENDED PLANTS

Acer griseum AGM
Paulownia tomentosa AGM
Liquidambar styraciflua 'Worplesdon' AGM
Solanum crispum 'Glasnevin' AGM
Clematis 'Niobe' AGM
Rosa 'Golden Showers' AGM
Buxus sempervirens AGM
Lavandula 'Grosso'
Hamamelis x intermedia 'Diane' AGM
Mahonia x media 'Lionel Fortescue' AGM
Viburnum x bodnantense 'Dawn' AGM
Rosa sericea 'Pteracantha'
Sambucus nigra 'Black Lace'
Cotinus coggygria 'Golden Spirit'
Pieris 'Forest Flame' AGM
Hydrangea quercifolia 'Snow Queen'
Agapanthus africanus 'Albus'
Nerine bowdenii AGM
Hosta 'Sum and Substance' AGM
Helleborus orientalis

The path curves on and through a circular colour garden, planted one side with hot colours and on the other with cool pastels. A timber pergola, clothed in clematis, roses and *Solanum crispum*, partially encloses the path as it passes through the colour garden. This leads on to a circle of gravel, surrounded by a prairie planting of ornamental grasses and herbaceous perennials. This is a more relaxed area and the grasses will be allowed to gently invade the gravel over time. A further seating niche complements this area. The third tree is a liquidambar, grown for its attractive foliage and vivid autumn tints. This dominates a border of choice shrubs including tree paeonies, hydrangeas and pieris.

Gardens owned by plant lovers often have an abundance (and possibly an excess) of plants, but with careful cultivation it is amazing how much can be grown in a small space.

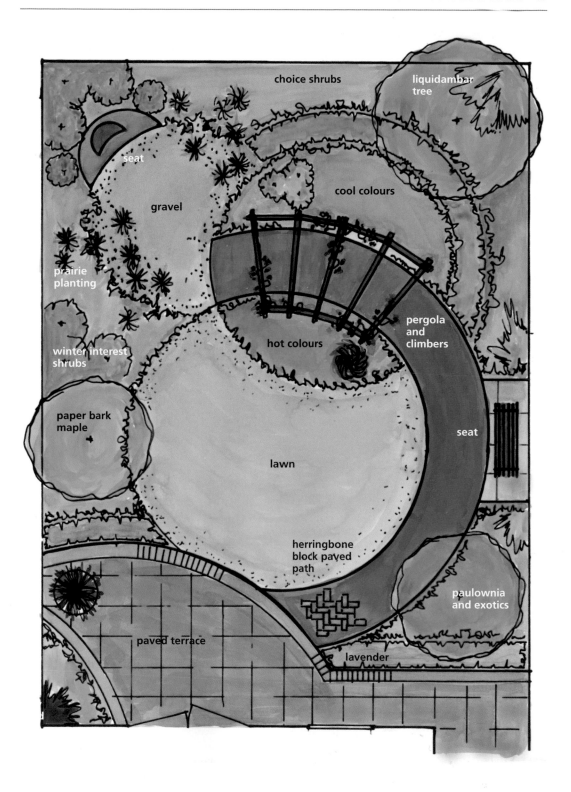

choice shrubs

liquidambar tree

seat

cool colours

gravel

prairie planting

hot colours

pergola and climbers

winter interest shrubs

paper bark maple

seat

lawn

herringbone block paved path

paulownia and exotics

paved terrace

lavender

THE EDIBLE GARDEN

This is a garden for those who like to grow their own fruit and vegetables but don't have much space. The design is formal, based on a series of rectangular beds. The raised beds are constructed from timber and give the ideal growing conditions for the basic vegetable groups: root crops, brassicas, legumes, onions, potatoes and tender vegetables. The borders at the side are filled with trained apples, pears, plums and cherries, underplanted with strawberries and herbs. A blackberry and kiwi fruit cover one wall, and a grape vine encircles a small arbour sheltering a corner seat. The seat faces a specimen tree, which could be any good ornamental tree but in this example a family apple tree is suggested; these trees have several types of apple grafted on the same tree to give a variety of crop.

Borders include soft fruits, asparagus and rhubarb. The greenhouse gives an ideal growing

RECOMMENDED PLANTS

Blackcurrant 'Ben Lomond' AGM
Whitecurrant 'White Versailles'
Redcurrant 'Red Lake' AGM
Gooseberry 'Invicta' AGM
Raspberry 'Glen Moy' AGM
Rhubarb 'Timperley early' AGM
Asparagus 'Conover's Colossal'
Family Apple tree
Pear 'Conference'
Plum 'Oullin's Golden Gage' AGM
Cherry 'Morello'
Kiwi Fruit 'Jenny'
Blackberry 'Loch Ness' AGM
Tayberry 'Medana'
Fig 'Brown Turkey' AGM
Strawberry 'Aromel' AGM
Rosmarinus officinalis
Laurus nobilis AGM

space for those tender crops such as tomatoes, cucumbers and peppers, and also for an early crop of strawberries to impress the neighbours! As these are responsible gardeners there are two compost heaps provided, and there is a water butt installed for recycling rainwater. An outdoor dining area is included with a table and chairs sheltered by the tree. The border near the house includes culinary herbs such as rosemary, bay, thyme, chives, parsley and coriander highlighted with wigwams of colourful 'Painted Lady' runner beans. The whole garden is surfaced with block paving to give easy clean access to the beds throughout the year, and also plenty of space for potted vegetables and fruit, such as the mini nectarine used as a focal point at the end of the central path.

A tiny walled garden, packed with productive fruit and vegetables, enhanced with some colourful artwork and a handy storage cupboard.

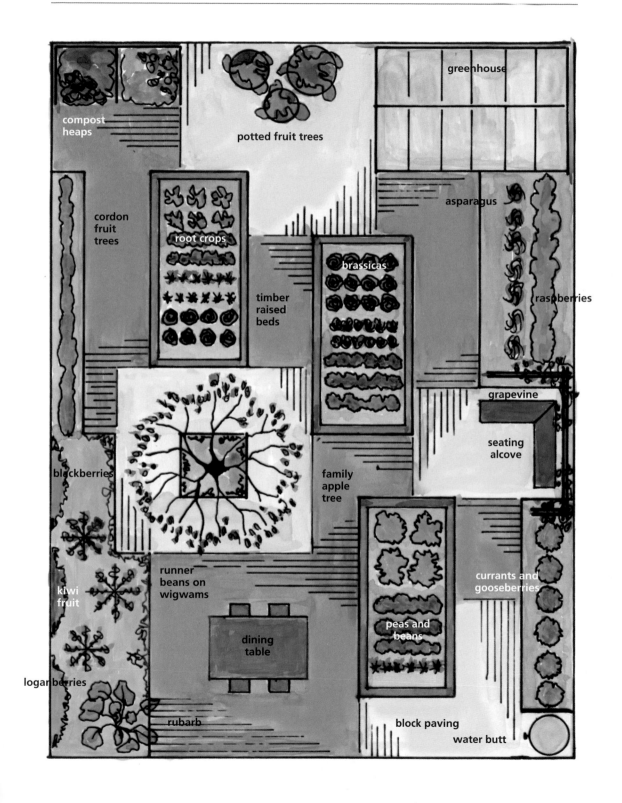

A LOW MAINTENANCE GARDEN

This small enclosed garden is innovative in style and would look good adjacent to a modern house. There is a large patio linked to a series of interlocking geometrically shaped areas of paving and blue slate chippings. The axis has been twisted in this garden so that the direction of the design leads the eye towards a small sheltered seating alcove in the top right-hand corner. The shapes of the spaces and the line of the stepping stone path both lead towards this corner. Different types of block paving contrast with the loose black slate chippings in the centre.

The garden is divided up with a series of short angled trellis screens that give some division to the garden so that it is not all immediately visible. The spaces between the panels each contain little surprises – a small piece of sculpture or a specimen plant. A progression of features leads the eye down the garden: the trio of planters on the main patio, then the seating cube at the edge of the gravel and on to the circular water feature. The seating area at the end of the garden is enclosed by a sheltering yew hedge and catches the morning sun, just the place for breakfast on a weekend morning. It looks back towards a piece of sculpture, hidden from the main garden by bold planting. The main patio will receive afternoon and evening sunshine and includes a barbecue and furniture for outdoor dining. Planting is permanent, using a range of groundcover plants, architectural specimens and ornamental grasses with the emphasis on low maintenance and a black and white colour scheme. A trio of white-stemmed birch trees gives height and light shade.

The colourful screens in this modern garden not only make powerful statements but also hide parts of the garden, encouraging the visitor to explore.

RECOMMENDED PLANTS

Betula utilis 'Grayswood Ghost' AGM
Fatsia japonica AGM
Phyllostachys nigra AGM
Phormium 'Platt's Black'
Sambucus 'Black Lace'
Viburnum tomentosum 'Mariesii' AGM
Pittosporum tenuifolium 'Irene Paterson'
  AGM
Cornus controversa 'Variegata' AGM
Cordyline australis 'Black Tower'
Vitis coignetiae AGM
Jasminum officinale AGM
Garrya elliptica 'James Roof' AGM
Heuchera 'Liquorice'
Ophiopogon planiscapus 'Nigrescens'
  AGM
Tulipa 'Queen of the Night'
Bergenia 'Silberlicht' AGM
Miscanthus sinesis 'Gracillimus'
Stipa tenuissima
Euonymus fortunei 'Silver Queen'
Lamium maculatum 'White Nancy' AGM

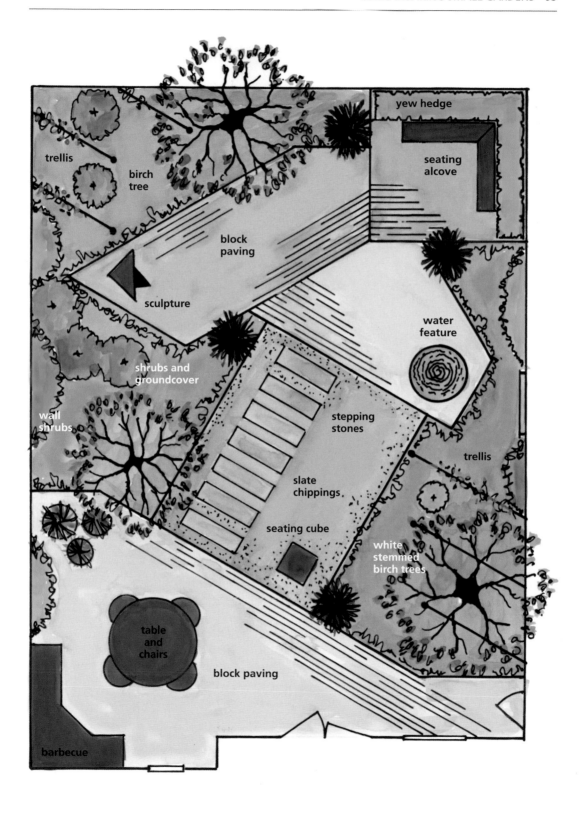

trellis

birch tree

yew hedge

seating alcove

block paving

sculpture

water feature

shrubs and groundcover

stepping stones

wall shrubs

trellis

slate chippings

seating cube

white stemmed birch trees

table and chairs

block paving

barbecue

THE COTTAGE GARDEN

The style here is traditional to match the old cottage that this garden adorns. This is also an example of a front garden, so very much a show space, designed to be both welcoming and attractive. The design is based on a series of curves, but to avoid being too formal the main footpath is offset from the front door and approached by a curving random York stone path, lined with a low lavender hedge. The sweeping lawn starts with a semi-circle and rustic seat to the right of the garden. The shape continues beyond the lavender walk leading in to a broader arc of lawn with a stone birdbath set in a York stone circle to one side. The lawn takes a turn and leads on through a rustic archway clothed in highly perfumed, dark red 'Etoile de Hollande' rose and framing a view to the distant countryside.

RECOMMENDED PLANTS

Apple 'Bramley Seedling' AGM
Prunus 'Cheal's Weeping' AGM
Rosa 'Wedding Day'
Peach 'Rochester' AGM
Rosa 'Étoile de Hollande'
Currant 'Red Lake' AGM
Gooseberry 'Careless' AGM
Rhubarb 'Champagne' AGM
Lathyrus odoratus 'Galaxy Mixed'
Cynara cardunculus 'Green Globe'
Runner bean 'Painted Lady'
Lavandula 'Grosso'
Dianthus 'Doris' AGM
Rosa 'Graham Thomas' AGM
Achillea ptarmica 'The Pearl' AGM
Alchemilla mollis AGM
Geranium 'Johnson's Blue' AGM
Hemerocallis 'Golden Chimes' AGM
Euphorbia characias 'Lambrook Gold' AGM
Kniphofia 'Royal Standard' AGM

An old 'Bramley' apple tree adds height and is swagged with white rambling 'Wedding Day' roses for summer interest. The borders are filled with a confection of flowering shrubs, scented roses, herbaceous perennials and bulbs. The emphasis is on simplicity and colour. Sweet peas scramble over a wigwam of hazel stakes, and two potted box bushes frame the front door, which is unashamedly traditional with more climbing roses scrambling over the porch. Here and there, fruit bushes mingle with the ornamentals, and gaps are filled with fast growing salad crops and herbs, creating a garden that is both attractive and productive.

Cottage gardens rely on a profusion of simple traditional flowers like the foxgloves, alchemilla and delphiniums growing in these borders.

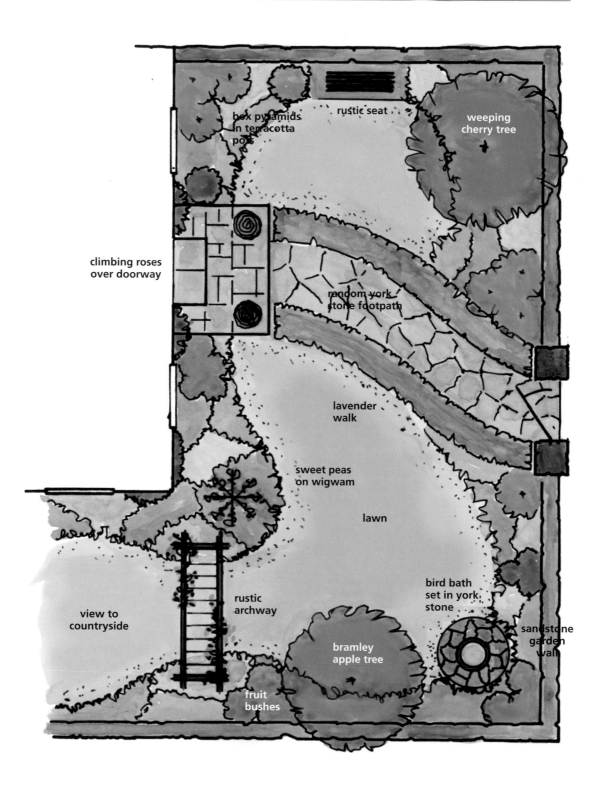

box pyramids
in terracotta
pots

rustic seat

weeping
cherry tree

climbing roses
over doorway

random york
stone footpath

lavender
walk

sweet peas
on wigwam

lawn

bird bath
set in york
stone

view to
countryside

rustic
archway

sandstone
garden
wall

bramley
apple tree

fruit
bushes

THE AROMATIC GARDEN

In this design, we have a garden that is visually attractive and has a theme of scented and aromatic plantings – it smells delicious! The layout is based around a series of overlapping squares of paving, set on a diagonal. Each of the squares looking down the garden is smaller than the preceding one, giving a sense of false perspective and making the garden look bigger than it really is. This is a very formal, almost symmetrical garden, and the main line of sight is straight down the middle, through each of the squares to a featured terracotta pot with a huge plant of scented angel's trumpets at the end of the garden.

At the centre of the garden there is a cross axis terminating with a cast iron seat set in front of a scented climber which looks straight across to a small wall-mounted fountain on the far wall. The absolute centre of the garden features a flowering thyme lawn and a square pergola, which spans the central area and frames the views of the garden from four directions.

The planting includes two pyramid *Pyrus calleryana* 'Chanticleer' for their spring blossom and autumn colour, and two scented *Buddleja alternifolia*. The deep red climbing rose 'Etoile de Holland' mingles with white *Jasminum officinale* on the pergola, and the seat is backed with honeysuckle. The central axis is emphasized by low box edging, leading to tall yew buttresses that frame the seat and wall fountain. The rest of the planting is a loose and generous confection of old English roses, scented shrubs and aromatic herbs, mostly in pastel shades. This is a garden to enjoy on a warm summer's evening.

Plenty of scent and repeat flowering from this strong growing and lovely old-style rose, called 'Chaucer' and bred by David Austin.

RECOMMENDED PLANTS

Pyrus calleryana 'Chanticleer' AGM
Buddleja alternifolia AGM
Jasminum officinale AGM
Lonicera periclymenum 'Belgica' AGM
Rosa 'Étoile de Holland'
Buxus sempervirens AGM
Taxus baccata AGM
Rosa 'Gertrude Jekyll' AGM
Rosa 'Mary Rose' AGM
Thymus serpyllum var. *albus*
Thymus serpyllum coccineus AGM
Nicotiana sylvestris AGM
Lilium regale AGM
Choisya x *dewitteana* 'Aztec Pearl' AGM
Viburnum x *bodnantense* 'Dawn' AGM
Brugmansia arborea 'Knightii' AGM
Salvia officinalis 'Purpurescens' AGM
Dianthus 'Mrs Sinkins'
Rosmarinus officinalis 'Severn Sea' AGM
Lavandula 'Grosso'

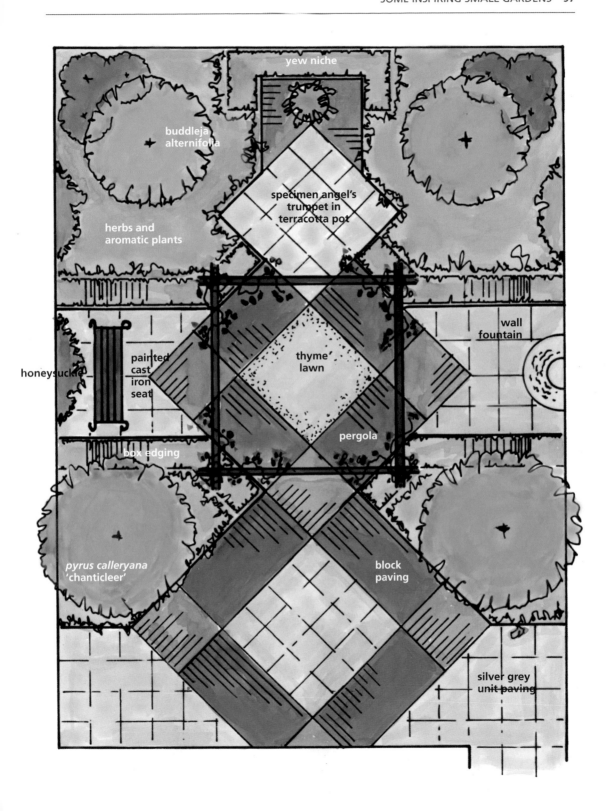

yew niche

buddleja
alternifolia

specimen angel's
trumpet in
terracotta pot

herbs and
aromatic plants

wall
fountain

honeysuckle

painted
cast
iron
seat

thyme
lawn

box edging

pergola

pyrus calleryana
'chanticleer'

block
paving

silver grey
unit paving

A MEDITERRANEAN GARDEN

This colourful garden is set on a steep slope which, rather than being a problem, has been used as an asset and the basis for three shallow terraces. The lower and widest terrace leaves plenty of open space for entertaining and includes a small fire pit for chilly evenings and some built-in benches with cosy cushions. A Chusan palm provides an exotic feature at the base of the steps. On the right of the garden a low wall made from rough timber, stained a rich burnt sienna, creates a raised bed filled with Mediterranean style planting such as cistus, rosemary and lavender dominated by a spreading acacia tree. A row of terracotta pots contain traditional red pelargoniums.

RECOMMENDED PLANTS

Olea europaea
Trachycarpus fortunei AGM
Pelargonium zonale 'Maverick Scarlet'
Cistus x *corbariensis*
Cistus x *pulverulentus* 'Sunset' AGM
Lavandula 'Grosso'
Convolvulus cneorum AGM
Astelia chathamica 'Silver Spear' AGM
Cytisus battandieri AGM
Fremontodendron californicum 'California Glory' AGM
Hebe 'La Séduisante'
Ficus carica 'Brown Turkey' AGM
Passiflora caerulea AGM
Phormium tenax AGM
Pittosporum tenuifolium AGM
Cordyline australis AGM
Artemesia 'Powis Castle'
Vitis coignetiae AGM
Grevillea 'Canberra Gem' AGM
Callistemon citrinus 'Splendens' AGM

Wide timber steps lead up to a second gravel terrace, with a small bubbling fountain amongst a heap of cobbles and boulders. Spiky leaved cordylines highlight the planting, which is backed by figs, ornamental vines and passion flowers on the surrounding walls. Wide stepping stones lead the eye to the next level where a hammock swings in a sheltered corner ready for use on warm days. The scene is completed with more planting dominated by a gnarled old olive tree, behaving like an aging diva and stealing the scene of the whole garden.

The terraces in this Mediterranean garden are packed with herbs, silver foliage and other sun loving plants that will relish the warmth and good drainage of this sloping site.

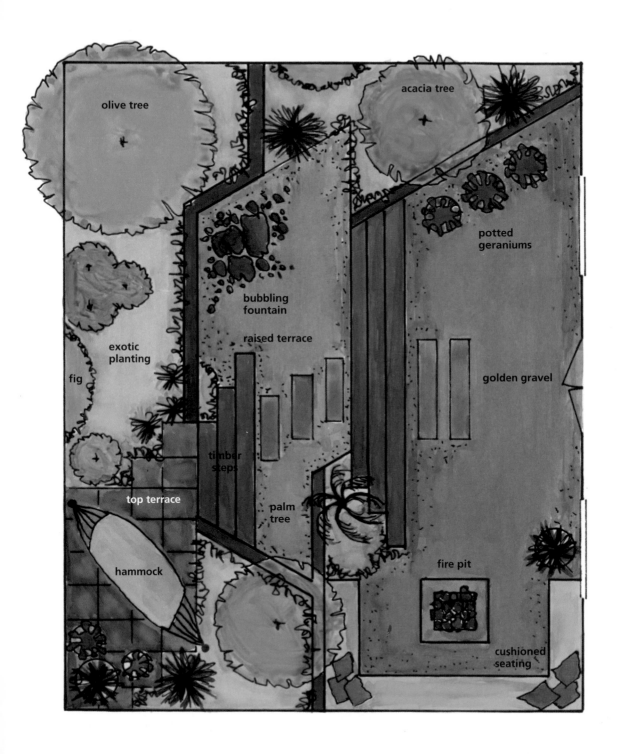

olive tree

acacia tree

potted
geraniums

bubbling
fountain

raised terrace

exotic
planting

fig

golden gravel

timber
steps

top terrace

palm
tree

hammock

fire pit

cushioned
seating

THE FAMILY GARDEN

This is probably a beginner's garden for a young family with limited experience and a tight budget but a desire to enjoy their garden. The space is simple and open, allowing easy access and a clear view for supervising small children at play. The wide angled deck gives a dry warm area for play and entertaining with a sand pit in one corner. The timber storage box will accommodate garden toys and double as seating. To one side of the decking there is a small herb garden and on the opposite side a space for a children's garden. This is accessible by stepping stones for easy culture by little people. The stepping stones continue through the lawn, leading the eye to the end of the garden where a metal obelisk covered in climbing roses acts as a focal point. Before this the stepping stones turn at right angles to a small partially hidden arbour. This can be either a 'secret' den for

RECOMMENDED PLANTS

Malus x *moerlandsii* 'Profusion'
Betula utilis 'Grayswood Ghost' AGM
Juniperus scopulorum 'Skyrocket'
Clematis montana 'Tetrarose' AGM
Vitis vinifera 'Purpurea' AGM
Lonicera periclymenum 'Belgica' Apple 'Katy'
Apple 'Discovery' AGM
Apple 'Fiesta' AGM
Philadelphus coronarius 'Aureus' AGM
Euonymus fortunei 'Blondy'
Escallonia 'Donard Star'
Cotoneaster horizontalis AGM
Buddleja davidii 'Nanho Blue' AGM
Forsythia 'Fiesta'
Cornus alba 'Aurea' AGM
Cistus x *lenis* 'Grayswood Pink' AGM
Hebe 'Great Orme' AGM
Pyracantha 'Orange Glow' AGM
Mahonia x *media* 'Charity' AGM

children or a parent's hideaway on a tiring day! Tucked at the end of the garden there is a small vegetable plot with enough room for some summer vegetables and salads. The opposite corner of the garden accommodates a child's swing, set in a thick layer of chipped bark to provide a relatively soft landing in case of accidents.

The borders are filled with a rich mix of flowering and foliage plants with the emphasis on ease of maintenance and year round interest. Two trees provide height and interest: a purple leaved crab apple for its flower and fruit, and a white barked birch with delicate foliage. A small pergola frames the stepping stone entrance to the lawn and is clothed with pink flowered clematis, an ornamental vine and sweet scented honeysuckle.

Colourful planting and a child's swing that looks attractive enough to be a garden feature, in this safe and simple family garden.

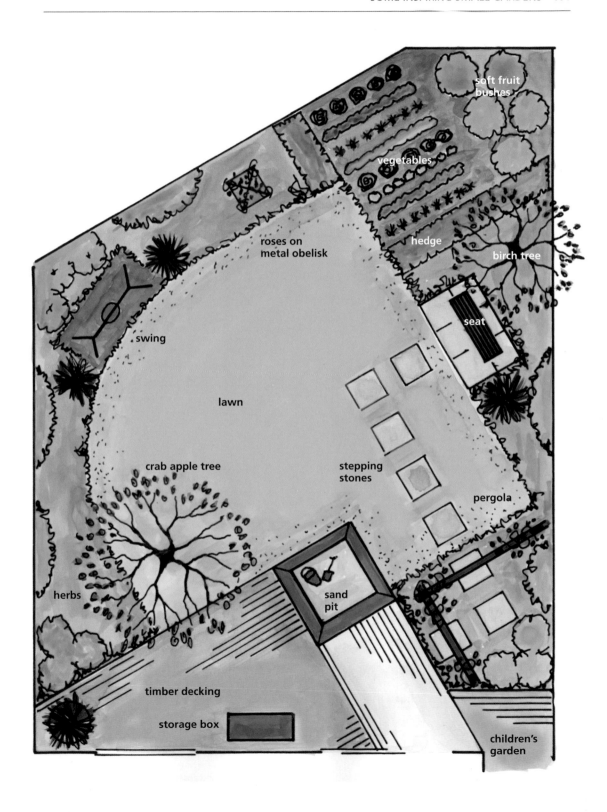

soft fruit bushes

vegetables

roses on metal obelisk

hedge

birch tree

seat

swing

lawn

crab apple tree

stepping stones

pergola

herbs

sand pit

timber decking

storage box

children's garden

THE MINIMALIST GARDEN

This contemporary garden sits behind a modern architect designed house. The scheme is based on a series of overlapping hexagonal shapes. The garden is approached from a small sheltered area of decking slightly raised above the garden level, with enough room for a small table and two chairs.

The main open space is a large hexagon paved in charcoal coloured block paviers and surrounded by architectural planting. Blocks of green bergenia, pachysandra and epimedium are accented with specimens of spiky *Phormium tenax* and the stately *Cornus contoversa* 'Variegata'. Giant black bamboos are set in octagonal containers amongst a carpet of loose cobbles. A climbing hydrangea

RECOMMENDED PLANTS

Pyrus calleryana
Morus nigra AGM
Phormium tenax AGM
Cornus contoversa 'Variegata' AGM
Phyllostachys nigra AGM
Fatsia japonica AGM
Hydrangea quercifolia AGM
Skimmia japonica 'Fragrans' AGM
Mahonia x *media* 'Charity' AGM
Aralia elata AGM
Hydrangea petiolaris AGM
Hedera colchica AGM
Miscanthus sinensis 'Gracillimus' AGM
Bergenia 'Silberlicht' AGM
Pachysandra terminalis 'Green Carpet'
   AGM
Epimedium x *rubrum* AGM
Festuca glauca 'Elijah Blue'
Nymphaea odorata minor
Iris pseudoacorus 'Variegata'

clothes one wall, and two plants of the large leaved *Hedera colchica* festoon the opposite boundary. Height is provided by a broken row of three fastigiated *Pyrus calleryana* 'Chanticleer' and a single specimen of mulberry near the decking.

The central block paving is angled to direct the eye from the decking across the garden to a water feature in the far corner. Two raised pools are set amongst lush foliage and framed by two of the pyrus. The water in the upper pool is aerated by a small fountain and then cascades over a waterfall into the lower pool. Waterlilies float in the still water at the pool's edges, and spiky marginal plants nestle into the corners.

Stepping stones cross a mysterious pool, set amongst green planting to an island terrace in this stylish formal garden.

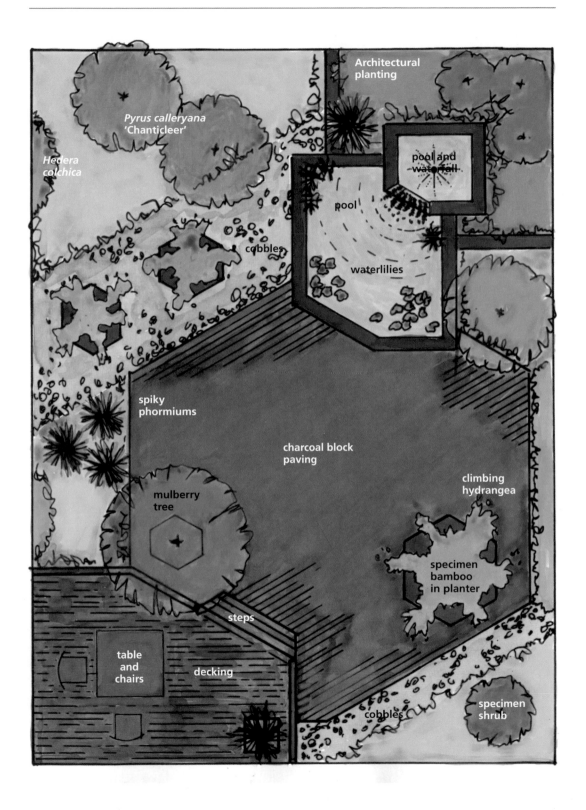

Architectural
planting

Pyrus calleryana
'Chanticleer'

*Hedera
colchica*

pool and
waterfall

pool

cobbles

waterlilies

spiky
phormiums

charcoal block
paving

climbing
hydrangea

mulberry
tree

specimen
bamboo
in planter

steps

table
and
chairs

decking

cobbles

specimen
shrub

A GARDEN FOR WILDLIFE

With increasing interest in environmentally friendly gardens, this plot incorporates many features to attract wildlife. The gravel area near the house allows for outdoor living, giving space for seats or a dining table, whilst allowing plants to seed and naturally encroach in an attractive way. A water butt is linked to the domestic rainwater system for water recycling, and a bird feeding station is near enough to the house for observation. A large informal pond will attract a variety of wildlife and includes a soft edge with a boggy area to allow easy access for frogs, toads and for young water birds when these nest in the area.

A mown path passes through a wildflower meadow towards a small spinney of birch trees and native shrubs. A broken path of log sections runs through the spinney to a small clearing with

RECOMMENDED PLANTS

Betula pendula AGM
Acer campestre AGM
Crataegus monogyna
Corylus avellana
Cornus alba
Euonymus europaeus
Ilex aquifolium AGM
Hippophae rhamnoides AGM
Ulex europaeus
Buddleja davidii 'Empire Blue' AGM
Lavandula angustifolia
Hebe 'Great Orme' AGM
Sedum spectabile AGM
Pyracantha 'Orange Glow' AGM
Aster x *frikartii* 'Mönch' AGM
Centranthus ruber
Helenium 'Moerheim Beauty' AGM
Cotoneaster horizontalis AGM
Berberis darwinii AGM
Digitalis purpurea

a log seat and a piece of recycled art. The habitat piles, logs and low level of maintenance in this garden all provide the right environment for a variety of wildlife. At the bottom of the garden there is a small plot for growing organic vegetables and two compost heaps to support this culture. The two borders that back the meadow and the pond are planted with a mix of native and cultivated plants with the aim of attracting birds, butterflies, bees and wildlife in general. This would also be an ideal garden for keeping bees and chickens. The wealth of nectar bearing plants would be ideal for bees, and chickens could roam freely without the owner worrying about damage to formal borders and lawns.

This tiny wildlife garden contains a bird nesting box and feeding station, a green wildflower roof, and some stylish timber sculptures, all set amongst vibrant wildlife plantings.

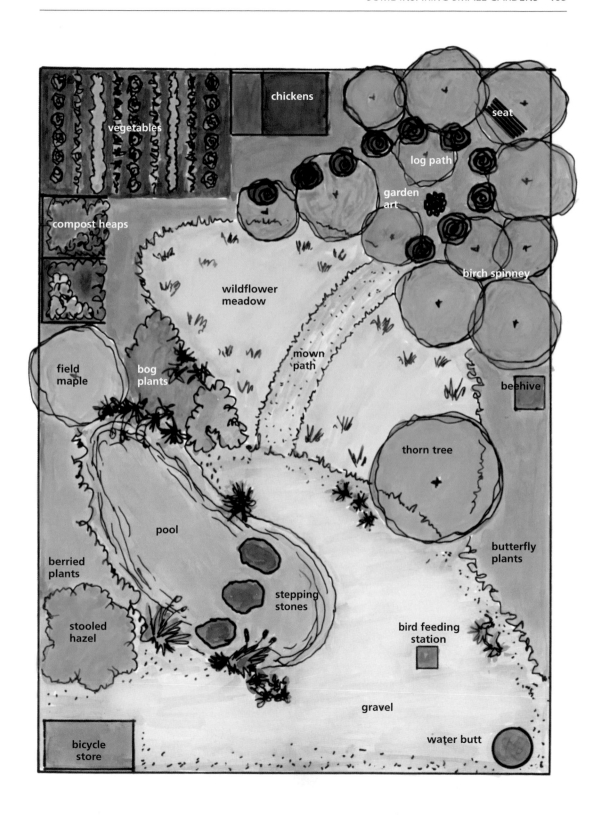

Room for a car as well as lush planting in this modest front garden, embellished with a metal sculpture and a green roof over the car port.

A CITY FRONT GARDEN

This little garden illustrates a number of the issues concerning small front gardens in city centres. In recent years much has been said about the problems of concreting over front gardens for car parking. The process reduces the percolation of water naturally into the soil and is so widespread that in some cities the water table has altered. Here we have allowed for an angled off-road car parking space on gravel hard standing. If properly constructed and treated with care, gravel will be economical to construct, permeable to rainwater and attractive to look at. Adjacent plants can naturally seed into this in an informal way, masking the fact that this is a driveway.

A block paved footpath leads to the front door. To soften the air of formality this has been set at an angle to the front door and linked with the drive. Block paving, when laid correctly on sand is also permeable and allows the percolation of water. A small enclosure constructed from chunky timber trellis and softened with an evergreen *Hedera colchica* hides a rubbish bin. This could equally be altered in shape to become a bicycle store.

Two trees give height and emphasis to the planting: a showy *Acer pseudoplatanus* 'Brilliantissimum' and a more muted weeping *Betula pendula* 'Youngii'. A fragrant *Trachelospermum jasminoides* climbs over a small trellis next to the front door, with some winter flowering *Iris unguicularis* at the base. A spiky *Phormium* 'Yellow Wave' completes this group. Underneath the bay window, the slow growing *Cotoneaster horizontalis* hugs the wall and will show off its brilliant red berries in autumn. The borders are filled with a mixture of architectural plants and groundcover for low maintenance. An informal bed of tough low growing groundcover is carefully positioned in the centre of the parking area to avoid the car wheels. The scheme is finished with a large terracotta pot containing colourful summer flowers and foliage.

RECOMMENDED PLANTS

Acer pseudoplatanus 'Brilliantissimum' AGM
Betula pendula 'Youngii'
Trachelospermum jasminoides AGM
Phormium 'Yellow Wave' AGM
Cotoneaster horizontalis AGM
Hedera colchica AGM
Iris unguicularis AGM
Hydrangea quercifolia AGM
Griselinia littoralis 'Variegata' AGM
Mahonia japonica AGM

Phlomis fruticosa AGM
Sambucus 'Black Lace'
Hakonechloa macra 'Aureola' AGM
Bergenia 'Ballawley' AGM
Pachysandra terminalis 'Variegata' AGM
Festuca glauca 'Elijah Blue'
Heuchera 'Plum Pudding'
Artemesia 'Powis Castle'
Alchemilla mollis AGM
Epimedium x *rubrum* AGM

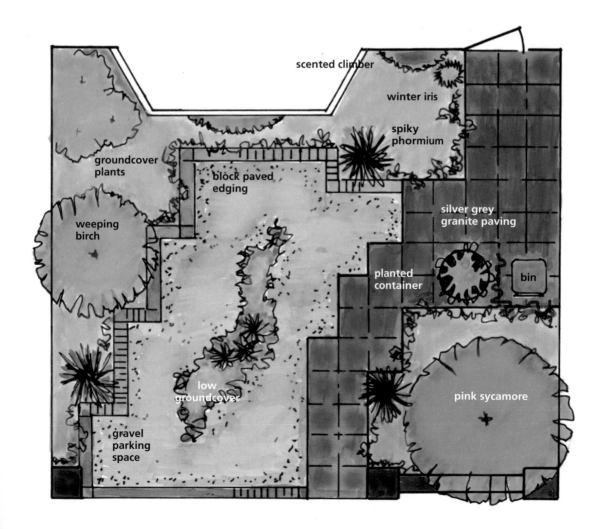

7 THE DESIGN BECOMES A GARDEN

Designing and constructing gardens are two totally different procedures, although both are creative and the two are obviously linked. It has to be said that the most spectacular gardens are those where the designer is closely involved in the construction, ensuring that what they imagined actually comes to be built and planted. So in a private garden situation, it is ideal if you can design your garden, lay the paving, till the soil and plant the borders. Then as you care for the garden year by year, observing it through the seasons with a critical eye, you can amend and alter to refine the results. Such a focused approach is highly likely to get excellent results.

HARD LANDSCAPING

So are you going to do the work yourself? If you tackle such work yourself you will undoubtedly be slower than the professionals and your back will ache at the end of the day, but the job satisfaction with the finished result will be high. Generally most hard landscaping (paving and walling) should be completed first, before you go on to creating borders and laying lawns. Get the heavy and messy work out of the way before you do the finer details.

Many tasks involved in garden construction are fairly basic. Laying paving, building steps and constructing basic retaining walls should not be beyond the means of most hobby gardeners, providing they take the time to find out how the

job should be done correctly. Certain aspects like using the right cement mortar mix in building a wall make the crucial difference between a successful feature and a crumbling mess a year later. Using the correct tools such as straight lines and spirit levels is essential for all construction work. Although this chapter will explain some of the basics of hard landscaping and planting, do get more detailed instruction if you are going to attempt skills you have not done before. Do also be aware of safety issues when using power tools, such as angle grinders to cut stone, and when handling heavy materials. Be sure to equip yourself with stout steel toe-capped boots, gloves, ear and eye protection. Ideally get a more experienced friend to guide and preferably share the job!

Landscape materials can be expensive so consider the costs and sources carefully. Most paving, bricks and hard landscape materials will be cheaper at a builder's merchant than at a garden centre, although some of the large DIY multiples can be very competitive. If you need topsoil, check local advertisements, as there is nearly always someone who needs to get rid of some. Reclamation yards are excellent sources for all sorts of things, not just artistic bric-a-brac but often old bricks, second-hand paving, gates, railings, ornamental stonework and rough timber. For mulch, search out a local sawmill to see if they produce their own. They may also stock tree stakes and poles suitable for pergolas. And of course there is the internet. It's amazing what can be found on eBay or Amazon – always worth a try! Aim also to buy plants from a nursery that grows their own, and you are more likely to get top quality fresh plants. For novelties and a wide selection, you will be best to search the local garden centres.

OPPOSITE: **A well-designed and constructed garden will not only give a great deal of pleasure but also add considerably to the value of the property it adjoins.**

Marking Out on Site

Marking out on site is an essential exercise whether you have planned your garden on paper or just in your mind, and regardless of whether you are intending to do the work yourself or hire a contractor. What looks correct on a drawing may not necessarily look exactly right on the ground, and you may need to make some changes to get the garden looking perfect on site. Plot in the key features of your garden using bamboo canes, stakes, string or whatever helps. A hosepipe can be used to mark potential curves, with tree stakes placed where you are considering planting trees. Stand a pair of step ladders where you might be putting a gate or trellis, and put

These paving slabs are being carefully laid on a bed of cement mortar over a compacted base of stone, and the whole area is edged by contrasting block paviers.

empty pots where key plants are due to go. Try to imagine what the garden will look like when constructed, planted and eventually mature.

Stand back and look at the arrangement you have created, trying to imagine how it will appear when established. Look at the composition from different viewpoints – key windows, your patio and conservatory, if you have one. You can then make small or large changes before you commit yourself to hard work and possible expense. Nothing worse than having planted a new tree only to decide later it's in the wrong place!

Laying Paving

You will have to excavate before laying paving, unless the ground is already lower than needed. Always make sure that the level of your paving adjacent to any buildings is at least 15cm (6in) below the damp proof course.

All paving must be laid carefully onto a well-prepared base. Brick paviers should be laid on a 50mm (2in) bed of compacted sharp sand, over a 150mm (6in) layer of a free draining material such as limestone scalpings. (This means a total excavation of 250mm (10in) to allow for all the layers.) Each layer must be compacted. Blocks are usually firmed in place with a vibrating plate, available from a hire store, and finished with dry filling sand brushed into the gaps. Paving slabs will also require a 150mm (6in) sub base to provide drainage. Ideally paving slabs are then laid on a 25mm (1in) bed of cement mortar; the slabs are gently tapped into the mortar until they are accurate.

Although rain may drain through the cracks between slabs and block paving, it is always wise to lay paved areas so that they slope in a sensible direction to shed water in heavy rain. You may be able to direct this towards an existing rainwater gulley or quite simply away from the house and onto lawns or adjacent borders. It stands to reason that if you are constructing driveways or areas which will be crossed by vehicles, you will need a much more substantial base and to be sure that the paving is adequate to take the weight of a vehicle.

Cobbles and gravel like this red porphyry should be laid on a landscape membrane to prevent weed growth and also avoid the soil from below working its way up.

Inspection Cover Problem?

Drainage engineers seem to delight in positioning inspection covers in the most prominent position – just where you want your patio, or right in the middle of a proposed lawn. These very necessary steel covers are never attractive. Think carefully about how you will try to hide it.

A potted plant placed on top of an inspection cover in the middle of your paving will only draw attention to the offending steel plate. Occasionally a planter may work, if the cover is where you would logically place a container of plants. Beware of using a large heavy container such as an alpine sink. Whilst it might well do the trick in disguising the cover, it could be very heavy to shift in the event of an emergency, when sewage has backed up and flooded your house!

Inspection covers in paved areas are best disguised when the paving is laid by installing a hollow cover. This is like a shallow metal tray in which paving can be laid to match your patio. The paving can be cut and angled to match the rest, and the thin steel frame becomes almost invisible. Inspection covers can be disguised with gravel or cobbles if this fits with the design, but do remember that you are masking them and, in an emergency, they would not be immediately located by anyone not already aware of their location.

In a lawn, the best treatment is to paint the existing cover a dark green and also not to trim around the edge but to allow the grass to mask the edges. Alternatively, you may be able to alter the shape of your lawn to hide the cover in a nearby border. Never turf or plant over covers, as they must be easily accessible. In a border, surround them with low growing spreading plants such as *Genista lydia* which can quickly be trimmed back if needed.

This pool has been constructed with a concrete base and substantial concrete block walls and will be finished with a waterproof cement render.

Creating Gravel Areas

Laying gravel requires minimal skills so is easily done, but barrowing large quantities of gravel can be hard work. You will need about 60kg/m^2 (1cwt/yd^2) for adequate coverage. Areas for gravel surfacing should be raked smooth and level, and then covered with landscape fabric, which is a porous woven black material. This will allow water to percolate through, prevent weeds from coming up from the soil below, and will also stop your gravel getting mixed with the soil and becoming muddy.

You may want to finish a gravel area with some sort of precise edging to prevent the gravel becoming mixed with the soil from the border next to it. You can use a timber edging or lay a single row of block paving. However with many gravel gardens you may wish for a more relaxed style and for plants to be able to creep gently into the gravel areas so that there is a harmony between planting and gravel. Prairie planting using ornamental grasses works very well with gravel areas; many of your grasses will seed naturally into the gravel.

Constructing a Water Feature

Garden pools can be very expensive to have constructed professionally and very satisfying if you do it yourself. Pools can be made of a variety of materials. Traditionally concrete was widely used and still is, but handling this requires quite a few skills, and if the process goes wrong you can end up with a very expensive leaking pond. Concrete is probably most suitable for formal geometric pools. Steel reinforcing mesh must be used in all sections, and you must ensure that the join between the base and the sides is strong. Pools should always have sloping sides so that any ice in winter can gently rise up as it expands. If this is forgotten, then freezing ice can crack even a concrete pool. A concrete pool must be finished with a single coat of rendering and a final coat of a waterproofing agent.

Fibreglass shells to create pools are available in all sorts of shapes and sizes. They look easy, but a hole must be excavated almost exactly the same shape and size as the shell. After positioning, the gap must be backfilled between the sides of the hole and the fibreglass. This loose soil must be thoroughly firmed so that when the pool is filled with water the fibreglass is supported rather than stressed; otherwise cracking and leaking may occur.

Probably the easiest and cheapest method of constructing a pool is by using a black butyl liner. Butyl is a tough rubber-like material. Start by digging out a hole exactly the shape, size and depth that you want your pool to be. This can incorporate different depths, shallow shelves for marginal plants and deeper levels for fish and deep aquatics. Butyl will also adapt to intricate informal shapes so you can be as creative as you want. If the digging looks daunting hire a small mini excavator; however do be sure that you are not going to dig through any cables or pipes by making some test digs by hand in advance. Try to plan the area around your water feature in advance so that you can reuse the excavated soil nearby. Getting rid of spoil can otherwise be very expensive and involve some very laborious barrow work.

When you have the shape excavated, thoroughly line it with either a thick layer of wet newspapers or soft sand patted into place; this is to cover over any sharp stones or odd pieces of metal that could puncture your liner.

Ensure that you calculate the size of your liner to allow for the size of your pool, plus the sides and a bit extra to overlap the edges. Now lay the liner loosely over the hole and roughly anchor it at the sides with a few bricks. Make no attempt to fit it to the shape but place a hosepipe in the centre and start running water. Allow the weight of water as it fills to gently pull the liner into the hole and you will find that it naturally stretches and folds exactly where needed. Finishing off a butyl-lined pool can be tricky. If using paving slabs, you just lay the slabs over the butyl overlap. For the more natural look carefully tuck the surplus butyl into the ground and then turf over the edges, making sure that the turf has soil to root into.

SOFT LANDSCAPING

Planting the Borders

Preparing borders for planting is a straight-forward gardening exercise, but remember that most permanent planting should grow and thrive without a major overhaul for five to ten years, so good thorough initial preparation is essential. All borders should be deeply dug, breaking up any compacted soil and incorporating good-quality organic matter and a high phosphate pre-planting fertilizer. Any specialist soil changes for particular plants should be made at this stage. Don't be tempted to cut the corners on hasty soil preparation.

Plant shrubs carefully in a good sized hole, ensuring that the root system is covered and well firmed in but not buried.

Always plant any trees first, taking time to make sure you have got them in the right locations. Staking young trees is a fairly essential procedure to avoid them rocking in the wind before a new root system has been established. In a private garden it is not usually too critical where the stake goes, so you can partially hide it behind the tree. Alternatively you can make it part of the initial design by painting it a bright colour to tie in with the rest of your scheme. Pot grown trees will have a large root ball which should not be disturbed, and it is preferable to support with a short stake driven in at an angle so that it avoids the rootball; the tree can be tied to the top of the diagonal stake. Always use the proper rubber tree ties that will expand and avoid strangling the tree as it grows.

The planting proceeds in the same way the design was created. Firstly plant any large specimen shrubs from big pots, then the smaller shrubs and finally herbaceous perennials. Do always lay out the plants for each area in their pots, stand back and look at the results before you actually dig the holes and plant the plants. Sometimes what you have planned doesn't look quite right when you go to plant it, but a little juggling between the plants and the spacing will usually give you a successful result. During the winter, when the soil is usually moist, there should be no need to water-in after planting. However, if soil conditions are dry, especially during the late spring and summer months, be sure to thoroughly soak all new plantings immediately.

Do try to finish off all planted areas with a mulch, which retains moisture for your valuable new plantings, reduces weed growth and generally gives a dark uniform soil finish. You can use a wide range of organic materials, but the most suitable for most gardens is composted bark. Do however obtain one of the better quality materials with a high proportion of bark and a low percentage of wood chippings. A bargain mulch, described as 'amenity landscape mulch' will be likely to have a high proportion of rough forestry waste and be more suitable for the landscaping in a supermarket car park, so best avoided.

This new planting scheme was mulched after completion and is growing away well during its first season, with virtually no weed problem.

Creating the Perfect Lawn

Lawns can be created either by sowing grass seed or by laying turf. Both will produce a high-quality lawn providing you choose the right materials to start with. Seeding is the cheapest option but will require a little extra preparation and the resulting lawn will take longer to reach maturity – particularly important if you want to use it quickly. Turfing will give you an instant lawn that will be available to use relatively quickly.

Preparation for both involves good cultivation and particularly attention to drainage. A badly drained lawn will be constantly wet, muddy and particularly prone to growing moss. Good deep cultivation is essential. If you have a heavy clay soil, it can be beneficial to add extra sharp grit to improve drainage at this stage. Ideally major cultivation for a new lawn should take place a few weeks in advance of completion to allow the soil

to naturally settle and avoid air pockets which will eventually slump, leaving an uneven lawn.

Final preparation will involve a combination of raking and treading. This should be done when ground conditions are relatively dry so that the soil crumbles easily. Raking will give you a smooth surface and also enable you to gather up large stones and other rubbish. Treading gently firms the surface, removing the air pockets. Trampling up and down on the soil you have just dug may get you odd looks from the neighbours, but it's the right way to do the job! Do not use a roller – ever! If you are using lawn seed, the final raking needs to be a little more precise and stone free, as this will be the ultimate lawn surface when the grass grows. Use a pre-planting fertilizer that will be high in phosphates and rake that into the surface.

Grass seed is best sown in the spring and autumn months. If your lawn is likely to get

Carefully laying rolls of lawn turf to ensure a strong contact with the soil beneath and no gaps between adjacent turfs.

heavy usage, choose a hard-wearing mixture which includes some fine leaved ryegrasses. Sow the seed very evenly at a rate of about $30g/m^2$ ($1oz/yd^2$). Don't be tempted to use more for a quicker result, as you're more likely to get crowded seedlings which will succumb to disease. After sowing, rake the seed lightly into the surface. After your young lawn germinates, allow it to grow until the grasses are about 5cm (2in) tall and lightly trim it back to about 2.5cm (1in) with a sharp lawnmower, being sure to remove all the trimmings.

If you opt to use turf, be sure to find a supplier of a good quality cultivated turf and ask to see a sample before you actually purchase. Turf is very variable and can be poor quality. Avoid anything described as meadow turf. Turf will be delivered directly to your house, and again check a couple of rolls before it is all unloaded to make sure that the quality is still good – an even dark green colour –and has not dried out during the delivery period. As you unroll each turf on the ground, make sure it is tightly butted against its neighbour and that there is no soil showing. Try to use full-size turves at the edges, and if there is a need for small fillers, make sure they are tightly butted between other pieces so that they do not come astray and dry out. Some gardeners like to work from a plank placed on top of the turf they have just laid; walking on the plank helps to firm the turf in place and also means that you do not have to walk on your freshly raked soil at any stage.

Newly laid turf must never dry out, so as soon as you have completed laying an area, make sure it has a thorough soaking, ideally with a sprinkler. In dry weather this should be repeated two or three times a day. In theory you can lay turf at any time of the year, but the summer is much trickier due to the risk of dry weather and high temperatures. If turf ever dries out it will shrink, gaps will appear and it won't recover without a lot of extra work!

RENOVATING AN OLD GARDEN

Old overgrown gardens can be wonderful starting points for a new garden, as you can usually retain and renovate parts of the existing garden. Consider the trees carefully, as they will often have taken many years to grow to their current size. If they are in proportion with the garden and you decide to retain them, they can often be improved with careful tree surgery. On a small tree you may do this yourself, but with any work requiring chainsaws or working above ground, always employ a qualified tree surgeon. Dead wood should always be removed from a tree for both tidiness and reasons of safety. A tree that has become a little too big can be reshaped by crown thinning, which leaves the natural shape but a little smaller by removing a proportion of the longest branches. Where the crown dips too low to the ground, this can be lifted by removing the lower branches. Never ever be tempted to pollard a tree (remove all its branches) as the shape will be

**The well-maintained lawn in this informal country garden is an important part of the
design, giving a neutral foil for the colourful surrounding borders.**

lost for ever and the stump will re-grow at twice the speed!

If you acquire a garden with an old overgrown hedge, you may find that it has spread and takes up far too much space. Providing the hedge is healthy, you can rejuvenate it and reduce it considerably in size. Most familiar species including yew and box will respond well, but conifers will not. The process takes two years. In the spring of the first year, reduce the hedge down to just below the height that you want and cut back on one side hard to the main framework, which will become apparent as you start to prune. Then feed, mulch and water during the following summer and the hedge should regrow strongly. The next spring you can repeat the procedure on the second side. Trim the new growths regularly to get a nice tight green barrier.

Existing paving needs to be assessed carefully. If paths or patios are in the right place, sound and level, you may be able to just clean the surface with a stone cleaner and maybe re-point the joints, and you will have an acceptable finish. However it is more than likely that much of the paving may have slumped or cracked. In this situation it may be worth lifting and stacking the good slabs, laying a fresh sub base and relaying the paving, maybe adding some new as needed.

Don't be afraid of colour! Paint is cheap and offers the opportunity to use colour in a variety of ways. Trellis and fencing can be almost any colour you like, not just creosote brown. Most wood preservatives are available in many bright shades. Garden furniture can be stained to match a nearby border or a favourite glazed garden pot. A

The fiery scarlet stain on these timber benches contrasts well with the surrounding green vines, but it could easily be painted over with an alternative colour if the owner tires of red.

blank concrete wall can be painted with stone paint, and if you get tired of the colour it can be repainted in another shade. However, do beware of painting good brickwork. It rarely looks attractive and is tedious to remove. Also think very carefully about strong colours in permanent materials such as new paving, which cannot easily be altered. Changes can be expensive or you will have to live with something that jars!

USING A CONTRACTOR

Many people will feel that whilst they have the design skills and the imagination to create an attractive scheme, they may not have the energy and time to actually do all the hard work, and this is where contractors become involved. You can use landscape contractors for all or maybe just part of your garden construction. For example, you may well be happy to do the planting, providing someone else does the paving.

Always obtain detailed, competitive quotations from at least three landscapers. Prices vary considerably. Ask to see the results of their work in other

The customer discusses details of this skilfully laid herringbone pattern of block paviers with the contractor.

As a garden matures and plants grow, skilful pruning will be essential to ensure that plants do not become too competitive or block paths or windows.

gardens and if possible speak to past customers. Beware of skimpy quotations lacking detail. Ask for details of what the paving will be laid on, depths of cultivation and materials to be used. Samples should be supplied if requested. There are cowboys in every trade, including the landscape business. Never accept a verbal quotation. Avoid any contractor who knocks at your door to offer their services, and be very wary of a contractor that can start tomorrow. Good contractors will be busy and have a waiting list. Always ask for a precise starting date and predicted completion date before placing your order.

When your selected contractor starts on site you need to both observe and monitor the work carefully but at the same time avoid interfering. You might ask to see critical stages, such as the depth of excavation before they start filling up with aggregate and laying paving. Arrange to be present on the day they are planting, so that you can see the plants laid out before they go in the ground. Juggling plants around is a five minute job, but asking for them to be dug up and moved after planting will not make you popular, even if the fault is theirs. It is always easier to correct a job that is going astray at an early stage than to complain when it is finished. Make sure that any instructions you give on site are always given to the supervisor, and back these up with an email to their office or keep a written list of site instructions. Always ask if anything requested will add an extra cost. Small things like cups of tea, and praise when the work is looking good, always help to keep things smooth.

Good contractors will always hold reasonable liability for the work they do. If anything goes wrong, such as paving cracking, lawns sinking or plants unreasonably dying, they should return to rectify the work without quibble. Ask about this at the quotation stage.

MAINTAINING YOUR GARDEN

Good gardens require love and care to ensure that they continue to grow and develop, getting better year by year. A garden that is neglected will soon start to look sad, and problems such as pernicious weeds that develop in a short while may be with you a long time, so try to give your new garden the attention that it deserves. The most demanding task of all in a garden is usually grass cutting, and if you do not want this regular commitment it is likely that you will have opted to avoid a lawn.

With almost all garden tasks, the most important requirement is to try and do things at the correct season. When you do this, the job is likely to be straightforward and the result to be most effective. Leave the job, and it often becomes more difficult, and you may miss the window of opportunity for certain seasonal tasks. If at all possible, try to spend an hour or so in your garden every week, whatever the season, and this will avoid a build-up of jobs – easy to say but not quite so attractive during the cold winter months! Although this book isn't really intended to be maintenance manual as such, there are some key points to observe when nurturing a new landscape.

Pruning in a Nutshell

One of the most important skills to learn is the correct way to prune plants and perhaps even more so, when not to prune. Far too many gardens are ruined by overzealous pruning. In general young shrubs and trees need very little if any pruning at all. With trees, look out for any double leaders. This is when a tree produces two strong competing main shoots and here, you should remove the weaker of the two. If any variegated trees or shrubs produce plain green shoots, these should be removed. Otherwise generally leave woody plants to establish on their own and they will naturally produce a pleasant balanced shape.

After a couple of years, some shrubs can be pruned to encourage their display. Some of them that flower in late summer, such as buddleja, caryopteris and ceratostigma can be hard pruned in the spring to encourage vigorous growth. Conversely those that flower in spring and early summer, including forsythia, philadelphus and kerria can be pruned by selectively removing the older flowered wood, as soon as flowering is completed. Dogwoods, members of the genus cornus, rubus and some willows, grown for their coloured winter stems, can be pruned down to ground level in late spring to encourage vigorous regrowth. Slow-growing evergreens such as rhododendron, camellia and also lilac should not be pruned at all, although you can remove the dead flower heads after flowering to avoid these going to seed and reducing the plant's vigour.

Eventually as gardens mature, plants that grow very well may start to smother their neighbours or cast too much shade, and so pruning becomes essential to reduce their size. Never ever use shears or hedge trimmers for this job as they will ruin the shape of your plants. Use sharp secateurs and prune selectively, cutting out 30–50 per cent of the longest branches but leaving the shorter branches untouched. In this way you will retain the natural outline of the shrub and hopefully still preserve some of its display in the coming season. If any shrub has really become far too big, you need to decide whether it is the wrong plant for that situation and whether it should be replaced with something smaller. If you decide to retain it, you can prune most shrubs hard back to stumps about 15cm (6in) tall and they will usually regenerate naturally, giving you several more years before they become a problem again.

Autumn Tasks

Be aware of the key seasons and tasks that need to be done to ensure your garden looks good in the future. In particular, plan displays of spring bulbs the previous summer, purchase in good time and plant in early autumn before the weather gets too cold and the soil wet and muddy. Tulips can be planted late autumn, but narcissus, hyacinths and most of the small bulbs should be planted in early

This small corner requires skilled maintenance including rose pruning, trimming of the box shape, slug treatment for the hostas and replanting of the annual flowers.

or mid autumn. At this time of the year you can also plant biennials such as wallflowers, polyanthus, and winter flowering pansies. Some of these will give a little winter colour during mild weather but then develop their main display in the spring months.

Sometime during the autumn, and particularly before the first frosts, you will need to prepare your garden for winter. Any tender plants which you want to keep for the next year must go into a frost-free greenhouse or a warm windowsill indoors. Pumps in water features and garden lighting can be left out all winter, but if you're unlikely to be using them it is prudent to pack them up and keep them clean and dry ready for next season. Pumps can get frozen in very severe weather, and excessive rain may creep into garden lights.

Any potted plants that are being left outside to overwinter should be tucked into a sheltered corner, and if they are at all on the tender side you should wrap the pots with insulating bubblewrap and place some horticultural fleece loosely around the top growth. Any tender roots such as gingers, cannas or dahlias that are being left in the ground should have a nice thick cushion of mulch placed over the roots. You may want to do some tidying up, such as pruning back herbaceous perennials that have finished flowering, but in general avoid too much pruning in the autumn. Some plants such as ornamental grasses

This little pond seems well established with a good mix of marginal plants and water lilies, but there are specks of duckweed visible which will soon spread and cover the entire surface if not removed.

look particularly fine as bronze skeletons, particularly when touched with winter frost. Don't forget to turn off the water supply to any outdoor taps, drain out the excess water and ideally wrap with some insulating material.

Mulching, Weeding and Feeding

If you find weeding a tedious job, make sure that you keep the mulch on your flower beds topped up each year. To be really effective, a mulch needs to be between 50–75mm (2–3in) deep; this will deter the emergence of most annual weeds. Keep a small spray pack of ready-mixed glyphosate handy to deal with any perennial weeds. This product is readily available, very safe to use and will kill most perennial weeds with a couple of applications. Do be aware that it will also kill anything else that it is sprayed on, so be very careful amongst a closely planted border and never use on a windy day.

To keep garden plants in tiptop condition and looking healthy, you should not neglect to feed them. Most borders of shrubs, roses and herbaceous perennials will respond well to a simple dressing of a compound fertilizer such as Growmore, applied in the spring at 60g/m^2 (2oz/yd^2). If you prefer to use an organic product, something such as blood, fish and bone will be equally effective but probably more expensive. During the summer months, you can encourage growth with particularly important plants – and especially with those in containers – by using a proprietary liquid feed, usually applied once a week.

Inevitably gaps will appear in your garden, where a plant has died or not grown as hoped. Regard gaps as an opportunity to try something new to keep your garden fresh and up-to-date. Most gardeners cannot resist impulse purchases, and it's a good excuse to indulge and buy a few plants when you see something that attracts you. You can keep such purchases in a small nursery corner, or pot them into attractive containers and use as temporary pot displays until you find a permanent home for them.

If there are particular jobs you do not like doing, try to find ways of completing them with minimum effort and in the shortest possible time. Nowadays there are many pieces of equipment that can be used to mechanize simple jobs. So for example if waste disposal is a problem in your garden, why not consider a small shredder which will rapidly reduce prunings to a heap of small fragments that can be easily composted. Small garden vacuums that will blow as well as suck make the job of collecting autumn leaves so much quicker and easier. Even simple techniques can often make a job much easier. Before you start pruning a hedge use a large garden sheet placed at the base of the hedge and it's a quick job to gather up the trimmings. If you are chopping back ornamental grasses, tie a piece of string around the whole clump before you start cutting, and all your waste stays in one bundle rather than being scattered as you trim.

Pond Weed

Although water features can be wonderfully rewarding, they can also be very demanding and need maintaining just as any other aspect of a garden does. New garden ponds that have been filled with tap water inevitably turn green in the summer with the growth of algae. This will reduce with time, but you can hasten this with various products available from aquatic suppliers; in particular there is a dark blue vegetable dye which can be safely added to ponds, reducing the amount of light entering the pond and therefore slowing down the growth of algae. You can also use bundles of barley straw wrapped in mesh bags and submerged just under the surface. Blanket weed, a particularly pernicious form of algae that makes long green strands, can be raked out to reduce the nuisance. Duckweed, a tiny aquatic plant less than the size of the nail on your little finger, proliferates rapidly in warm conditions. If you see small quantities in your pond, take a fine mesh net and try to remove it all thoroughly; allow it to establish and spread and it's virtually impossible to remove. Always check new aquatic plants when purchasing to make sure you're not importing this by mistake as a stowaway.

THE DESIGN GROWS

During the first year new planting schemes can seem a little slow, but the main emphasis should be on encouraging good strong root systems. The second season will usually show some vigorous top growth on new plants, but it will usually be between three to five years before a new garden really looks mature. During those early years of a new garden, you will probably be tempted to add some annuals, bedding plants or extra herbaceous perennials to help fill out the garden. This is a great stop-gap but do be careful that the temporary planting doesn't smother and slow down the growth of shrubs and other permanent plants. As the permanent planting starts to fill out, be sure to remove competing plants that you may have used as short-term fillers. Some gardeners, and particularly professional landscapers, will plant shrubs quite thickly to get an instant effect. There is nothing wrong with this, providing you monitor the growth as time passes and thin out to allow permanent plants to reach their mature size. In particular ensure that any shrubs that are grown especially for their shape, such as the tiered Viburnum tomentosum 'Mariessii', have enough room to develop and show off their mature profiles. With care, any surplus shrubs can usually be moved to another location to fill in or develop a new scheme.

ONGOING DESIGN

Once you have designed your garden, drawn the plan and done all the hard work, you can certainly start to enjoy your garden as it grows. However, great gardens are never finished. Unlike other art forms, gardens are not static but are living, dynamic and complex creations that continue to change as they mature. Although an artist may lay down his brushes, gardeners cannot put away their tools! Because of this, you can continue to use your design skills, amending, altering and improving your garden over the years. As an observant and critical gardener, you will undoubtedly be aware of which parts of your garden are successful and which areas could be better. At the same time, when you visit other gardens you will come back with memories of features you have liked, or planting combinations that have caught your eye. Store up such ideas for improving parts of your garden at the appropriate season.

For example you may have seen a new colour scheme of rich ruby shades with white and silver. Possibly you already have a nicely maturing specimen of the rich purple-leaved Cercis canadensis 'Forest Pansy' with nothing more than some rather overgrown ivy as ground cover. You could clear the ivy out and underplant with silvery perennials such as the variegated Brunnera 'Jack

Foxgloves make excellent fillers for new planting schemes and although they are not perennial will seed and readily provide another generation.

Frost' and spiky Miscanthus 'Cabaret'. If space allows, complement this with other shrubs such as the snowy-leaved Philadelphus coronarius 'Variegatus' and the new evergreen Photinia 'Pink Marble' with green leaves splashed with white, pink and ruby. Countless new planting schemes can be created around existing plants as your garden grows and develops.

It may also be that the emphasis of your garden changes, as it grows. Possibly a shrub that you planted some years ago, such as a magnolia, has been growing slowly and finally become a really striking specimen but is hidden amongst other planting. You may well want to remove the surrounding planting, to reveal it and replace with low-growing ground cover or even, in some situations, to alter the layout of the garden so that such a specimen can be presented in a setting of gravel or close mown grass. This in turn may alter the dynamics of your garden, suggesting the location for a new seat, so that you can sit and admire your newly revealed feature. Sometimes the way a garden grows dictates its own design. Rather than constantly pruning back a strongly growing shrub and spoiling its shape, it may well be better to change the shape of the border by altering the grass edge to allow natural growth.

Time, plant growth and general usage of the garden may also suggest alterations to the surfaces you originally created. Over time, maturing trees and shrubs will cast a certain amount of shade, and grass will tend to be less successful in a small garden, becoming weak, mossy and muddy. In such a situation you may well want to consider gravel as an alternative. Grass paths on regular routes may also sustain too much wear and a better permanent solution may be to design a paved path as an alternative.

Cold winters and other disasters may cause losses and damage to your garden, which will inevitably cause disappointment. However, such situations can always be seen as opportunities for altering and improving your garden. Since the original planting, there may well have been new plants that have been introduced that you would like to try. Gaping holes in your planting will give you the opportunity to plant something new,

either individual plants or possibly new groups. Even if everything grows perfectly and you have no losses, there is usually room for adding some finer detail. Extra bulbs, both for spring and summer display, can usually be squeezed into almost any garden between your permanent planting. And bulbs can often add a totally different feeling. For example, you might try planting spring bulbs in pastel shades, pale blues, primrose, pink and white in a border that will later on be resplendent in hot colours. Such a cool, gentle start to the season will help to emphasize the razzmatazz of the later summer display.

All such changes can be improvements to your original design and mean that the garden is always changing and improving. Some of the greatest gardens in existence were created many years ago. They may have changed considerably from the original design, having been altered and improved by various generations of gardeners that have owned them and tended them. But where gardens are lovingly tended, they get finer as the years go on.

As the exuberant planting in this fascinating garden has developed, the owner has removed the grass and replaced with wide gravel paths.

8 SMALL PROJECTS FOR GREAT GARDENS

If you have reached this point in the book, you will have discovered some of the challenges and rewards of designing a small garden. You may find that you don't need the full makeover but just something to jazz up an existing garden. The following selection of mini projects will give ideas for creating new features or dealing with problem spots. Most of them will also fit into the major designs in Chapter 6, and you may wish to slot one of these projects in, rather than something already proposed. So for example, the mini water garden could easily be used on the patio of the planter's garden instead of the hot bed.

Many people who only have a balcony, a front porch or a basement yard still yearn for a garden and some living plants. Some of these projects may be enough on their own for the space you have. In such a situation, every inch of space is precious, and you will consider carefully what you choose to grow and build. A tiny basement garden might still have room for some planted pots, a mini water garden and some herbs in containers. Such situations will have challenges of their own, balconies often being windy and basement yards being dark and shady.

These little schemes can be a fun way of learning new skills such as laying paving or building walls. Sourcing the materials and tools and practising the skills in just a small area can lead on to more ambitious projects at a later date. Even if you make some mistakes, rectifying on a small scale is likely to be fairly easy and not too costly. You can also try out ideas such as colour schemes on a small scale. A planter filled with rich cerise pink and lemon yellow flowers will be either an instant hit or a disaster to be quietly forgotten. If it's good you can expand the theme to a whole border next year.

Most of the projects can be completed at any time of the year. Whilst major replants and laying new lawns should be done during the cooler winter months, projects such as these are fun challenges to enjoy whenever the inspiration strikes. Most of these are planting projects, and the plants needed are most likely to be available in garden centres and nurseries in the spring and summer months. Even in the heat of summer, projects on a small scale can easily be kept watered if the weather is dry.

Small projects can also be short-term seasonal features. Perhaps you've picked up some mossy roots in a woodland. Use them in a shady corner together with some potted woodland plants such as heucheras, hostas and some ferns. Add pine cones and maybe a small piece of garden art and you have an impromptu garden feature. Enjoy it for a season or whilst it looks good and then change for something new when inspiration strikes again.

OPPOSITE: **This wonderful feature wall needs some skills to construct, but it is not a large project and might well be an attractive challenge for a hobby gardener wanting to learn new techniques.**

PLANTED POTS

A large container, planted with an exciting range of plants is like a small, very special flower bed. Such containers will often be intended to act as a focal point and so should be carefully designed to look exquisite. Buy the largest pot available that will fit in the location intended. The choice of a container will be entirely personal, but large terracotta pots are usually effective and fit in with almost any style of gardening. Put some loose drainage material in the bottom of your pot. Then fill your pots with a good quality John Innes potting compost, ideally JIP3. This is a traditional growing medium which includes some soil and will give stability and steady nutrition for a long-lasting display. You can add some water-retaining granules if you wish.

The summer display will be planted as soon as all danger of frost has passed in early summer. You may have a colour scheme in mind, or alternatively take a trip to a garden centre. Pick out a selection of plants that attract you and put them into your

An unusual foliage planter using a dark leaved phormium, the silver succulent *Kleinia repens* and the wonderful rich lustre of *Tradescantia* 'Purple Sabre'.

PLANTS FOR POTS

Summer display
Miscanthus sinensis 'Cabaret'
Ricinus 'Carmencita Red'
Heuchera 'Crème Brûlée'
Begonia 'Pin Up Flame'
Argyranthemum 'Butterfly' AGM
Ipomoea batatas 'Blackie'
Winter display
Cornus sanguinea 'Midwinter Fire'
Fatsia japonica AGM
Skimmia japonica 'Rubella' AGM
Hebe pinguifolia 'Pagei' AGM
Hedera helix 'Jester's Gold'
Hyacinthus orientalis 'Distinction'
Tulipa 'Queen of the Night'

trolley and see how they look together. Include some tall plants to give height, some foliage plants, a range of reliable flowering plants and then some low trailing plants to soften the edge of the container. Most of these plants are likely to be available amongst the bedding or patio plant range, but other foliage plants, grasses and herbaceous perennials may also make excellent container plants. Plant your container generously, much closer than you would with a flower bed, and this will give you a display which will absolutely burst out of your pot, full of colour and appeal.

Remember that containers must be watered regularly in dry weather and may need additional liquid feeding when the initial feed runs out. Dead-head any flowering plants as the blooms fade to keep new flowers coming. In the autumn you can replace your display with a fresh batch of plants to give winter and spring interest. You can use traditional spring bedding plants such as polyanthus, pansies and wallflowers, but these tend to be very short in stature and have minimal winter impact. Choosing a selection of evergreens and spring bulbs will give a long-lasting display right the way through until next summer. Any shrubs or herbaceous perennials can be moved on to the garden after use in containers.

HERB GARDEN

Any adventurous cook will know the value of fresh herbs in flavoursome cooking. Herbs are also quite ornamental, and even if you don't pick them it can be fun the tweak their leaves or run your hand through the aromatic foliage. Logically a herb bed should be near the kitchen and easily accessible so that you can pick a few sprigs of whatever you need without a long walk and getting your shoes muddy in winter. Small borders, raised beds, troughs and pots are ideal for herbs. Most herbs are herbaceous perennials or small shrubs so will last for a number of years after planting, but a few such as parsley, coriander and basil are annuals and need to be sown fresh each year.

Many herbs come from Mediterranean areas so need a warm, sunny and sheltered site to perform well. Prepare the soil as you would for any other planting scheme. Spring is a good time to start a herb garden as your local garden centre should have a wide range of herbs available in small pots, which are generally inexpensive. Bay and rosemary make quite sizeable shrubs so give them plenty of space to grow. Some herbs such as mint, sage and thyme are also available in coloured leaved forms, and these provide extra garden interest whilst being just as edible. With parsley, coriander and basil, you can buy young plants each year or sow your own seed in mid spring. Basil is tender so do not plant out until after the last frost. A few herbs, such as the mints and lemon balm are very invasive and should be grown in pots to curb their enthusiasm, although these can be sunk into the ground. Impressive trained bay trees in various fancy shapes are available to complement your displays of the humbler herbs.

There are many different ways of growing herbs such as this spiral bed here, but beware of slugs hiding under the surrounding slate.

SOME TASTY HERBS	
Melissa officinalis 'Aurea'	Golden lemon balm
Allium schoenaprasum	Chives
Anthriscus cerefolium	Chervil (annual)
Coriandrum sativum	Coriander
Anethum gravaeolens	Dill
Origanum vulgare	Marjoram
Mentha suaveolens 'Variegata'	Pineapple mint
Petroselinum crispum	Parsley
Rosmarinus officinalis 'Severn Sea' AGM	Rosemary
Salvia officinalis 'Purpurascens' AGM	Purple sage
Ocimum basilicum grow from seed	Basil
Thymus citriodorus 'Aureus' AGM	Golden thyme

ALTERNATIVE LAWN

Some of you may like the idea of a verdant green open space in your garden but without all the hassle of mowing a traditional lawn. You can then consider some of the alternatives to grass, which can be very effective in a small space. Probably the best known is chamomile, a low green carpeting plant with a very pleasant fragrance. The best form to use is the cultivar sold as 'Treneague' which is quite compact growing and doesn't flower. Although nowhere near as tough as grass, chamomile will nevertheless take some wear, so you can walk across a chamomile lawn. You can also try the very low growing forms of thyme, cultivars of *Thymus serpyllum*. As well as providing a green carpet, they will flower each summer and are available in various shades of white, pink, through to almost red. Although less tried and tested, there is no reason why you cannot try other very prostrate plants such as the silvery *Raoulia australis*, the fragrant *Mentha requienii* or *Arenaria balearica* which bears white flowers.

Establishing small lawns like this is fairly straightforward, providing you observe a few guidelines. All the species mentioned prefer full sunshine. The soil should be prepared in the normal way but needs to be as free of competing weeds as possible. Ideally prepare the soil well in advance and allow the weed seeds present to germinate. You can then hoe or spray off the resulting weeds, leaving a clean surface. If you do this two or three times, you will considerably reduce the amount of weeds likely to appear in future. At the same time buy plants well in advance, grow them on and then divide to produce a larger batch of smaller plants. You will get much better coverage and a more even sward by planting small divisions at say 15cm (6in) apart rather than large plants at 30cm (12in) apart. Keep your new lawn carefully weeded, water in dry conditions and you will soon find that the plants will spread and join. Such lawns will need an occasional trim, and particularly flowering species such as thyme will need to be lightly sheared after flowering.

In this example, chamomile has been used in an effective pattern together with stone paving slabs, giving a green surface and easy access to the raised beds.

ALPINE SINK

Rock gardens are generally unconvincing in a small garden but if you fancy growing some alpine plants, a small raised bed or an alpine sink may be just the thing for you. Alpine plants generally take up very little space, so quite a few can be grown in a small area, making them ideal for confined gardens. You can buy a purpose made alpine sink carved from natural stone or you can make one with a mixture known as hypertufa. This consists of two parts Portland cement, three parts sifted peat, three parts of sand or if you want a lighter weight product, use perlite. This is moistened to a thick mix. You will need to construct a double box with a thin cavity into which you can pack the moist mix. After you remove the mould, you can soften the edges with a wire brush and drill drainage holes in the base. Allow the new sink to thoroughly dry before you fill and plant.

Alpine plants must have excellent drainage so line the base of the sink with stones or rubble and then top up with John Innes potting compost No1 mixed with 50 per cent extra grit. A wide range of alpines will be available in the spring. If you choose to add dwarf conifers, make sure these are genuinely slow growing species not just young plants of some monster conifer. After planting your selected plants, carefully position some small pieces of rock and finish with a thick mulch of gritty chippings to keep the rootrun cool and moist. You can add small bulbs such as *Chionodoxa, Scilla* and *Crocus* in the autumn. Keep alpines watered in dry weather. Although most are very tough, anything with furry or grey foliage may suffer in wet winters, so you can protect them with a sheet of sloping glass positioned to shed the worst of the winter rains.

EASY ALPINES

Dianthus deltoides AGM

Lewisia cotyledon AGM

Cyclamen x *hederifolium* AGM

Phlox douglasii 'Crackerjack' AGM

Primula auricula AGM

Sempervivum tectorum AGM

Sisyrinchium graminoides

Rhodohypoxis baurii AGM

Juniperus communis 'Compressa' AGM

Oxalis adenophylla AGM

This beautiful *Lewisia* 'Little Peach' is thriving along with other alpines, giving a mass of colour and interest in this tiny alpine sink garden.

ESTABLISHING A CLIMBER

Planting a climber may seem a very basic task, but there are a few tips which will help the success and quick establishment of a new plant. Climbers are often used against a wall, tucked amongst other plants or intended to climb through an established tree. Whatever the situation, the new plant needs the best chance of growing well without undue competition.

If you're planting against a wall, make sure that you do not put the root ball closer than about 30cm (12in) from the wall. The soil adjacent to a wall is likely to be in a rain shadow and usually very dry and impoverished, so plant away from the wall and lean the top of the plant in towards the trellis or support. The same principle applies when planting climbers to scramble through trees. If at all possible avoid planting right close to the trunk of the tree, where the soil will be highly compacted and full of roots. If possible plant a climber out at the edge of the tree canopy and lead the plant into the tree with a bamboo cane. You can often do this on the back of the tree so that it doesn't look too odd.

Do find out how a climber supports itself, so that you can give it the best possible opportunity to cover the space allotted. Climbers such as ivies and Virginia creeper will cling well to brick walls once they attach themselves. Use a couple of bamboo canes to press the stems gently against the wall so that as they grow they can easily latch on. Climbers that have tendrils or twist their stems will need relatively slender supports around which they can easily twist themselves. Bamboo canes, wires, strings or thin stems of other plants usually work well. But if you want such a climber to work its way up around the smooth poles of a pergola, you will have to either add some strings, or wrap the pole with some plastic mesh. Climbing and rambling roses support themselves naturally by sending out long whippy stems that eventually drop under their own weight and then catch on the nearest object using their thorns. This is unlikely to be suitable in most garden situations, so you will need to tie in the new stems to the support as they grow.

You can get some quirky effects by planting more than one climber in the same location. Ivies mix well with deciduous climbers, and their colourful evergreen foliage can be very welcome in the winter. As well as all the woody perennial climbers we have spoken about, there are some fun fast-growing annual climbers. *Cobaea scandens*, the cup and saucer vine, *Eccremocarpus scaber*, the Chilean vine and *Ipomoea lobata* can all be easily produced from seed each year and should flower by midsummer. They are very useful for planting alongside bamboos and other evergreens. They grow rapidly giving a filigree of extra foliage and colour over the more sedate permanent residents and rarely become a nuisance as they usually die with a frosty winter.

When planting two clematis together for a contrasting effect such as this, be sure to plant cultivars that both require the same pruning regime.

KNOTS AND PARTERRES

Many people will have seen these in historic landscapes. The knot garden originated in the sixteenth and seventeenth centuries as a formal geometric pattern, usually of box hedging, interspersed with coloured gravels and sometimes simple flowers. A parterre was usually more elaborate, consisting of big swirling patterns of different interlinking clipped plants, and it was revived in the nineteenth century as part of the craze for formal displays with bedding plants.

The style can still be used today, particularly where a formal green garden is wanted, with the emphasis on interesting shapes and patterns. It must be executed precisely and must be well maintained to retain the crispness of the design. The species to use is *Buxus sempervirens* 'Suffruticosa', a dwarf form of the common box which does not grow too vigorously. Design the layout of your knot garden carefully, aiming for a simple clear geometric pattern. Purchase small plants and space them about 15cm (6in) apart. Young plants should establish and grow quickly at this spacing and will soon join together to give you the pattern you have planned. As they grow,

lightly trim even if they haven't reached the intended size, as this will encourage the growth to be compact and the hedges ultimately to be well clothed. When well-established, box should be trimmed at least once a year and preferably twice, using lines and straight edges to be sure that you get a clean precise geometric pattern.

Sadly box is affected by disease called box blight which causes browning, dieback and eventually death of the plants. If you do not wish to take the risk of this occurring, there are other species which can be used for a knot garden. *Pyracantha coccinea* 'Red Cushion' is another dark leaved evergreen with red berries, or you could try *Hebe subalpina* which also gives small white flowers in late summer. Lavender is well known for its blue flowers and silvery foliage and you should choose a compact cultivar such as 'Hidcote'. *Santolina chamaecyparissus* will also give you silvery foliage and should be trimmed hard each spring. Both of the latter will give a softer effect than close trimmed box. There is no reason why you cannot use a mixture of the different species, for different parts of the pattern, winding them amongst each other.

This box knot garden will need trimming at least twice a year to maintain clean lines and perfect geometric shapes.

'PINT SIZED' WATER GARDEN

Every garden, even small ones, can benefit from the charms of a water feature if carefully designed. Tiny bubbling fountains can be operated from very small reservoirs, hidden under a pile of cobbles and boulders.

You may want something, however small, that looks a little bit more like a pond and contains some aquatic life. Tiny mini ponds can easily be constructed in a watertight container. You can simply use a ceramic pot, a plastic container or a wooden half barrel. If there is any doubt about the container being watertight, be sure to use a waterproofing paint right at the beginning. A suitable size container is 45–60cm (18–24in) wide by at least 30cm (12in) deep. Choose an open sunny situation for a mini pond as most aquatics like sunshine, and once a container is full of water and plants, it will be too heavy to move easily.

Line the base of your container with about 5cm (2in) of loose gravel, a suitable environment for many aquatic creatures. Select aquatic plants that are not too vigorous, choosing a range including some taller spiky plants, maybe some flowering plants and also some underwater oxygenating plants. There are a number of miniature water lilies which will grow in very shallow water and are quite suitable for tub water gardens. You may also like to try floating plants such as water hyacinth and water lettuce, which although tender are very attractive for the summer months. Pot them up into small aquatic pots using a heavy clay potting soil, sold specifically for aquatic plants. Finish each unit with a layer of gravel which stops the soil floating away and making the water muddy. Circular aquatic pots are usually easier to fit together than square ones and if you cannot get these, use ordinary flowerpots, but drill some extra holes in the sides as well as the base. Providing your tiny pond has at least 40 litres (10gal) of water then you can include some small fish. Although restrictive, this is no more so than an indoor aquarium, although you will need to be aware of crowding as the fish grow.

COMPACT AQUATICS

Canna 'Erebus' AGM

Thalia dealbata

Juncus effusus 'Spiralis'

Sagittaria latifolia

Mentha aquatic

Pistia stratiotes

Eichhornia crassipes

Cyperus papyrus 'Nanus' AGM

Acorus gramineus 'Ogon'

Myriophyllum aquaticum

Nymphaea 'Pygmaea Helvola' AGM

Nymphaea 'Joanne Pring'

A simple wooden barrel has been used as a mini pond for growing aquatic plants including this spectacular insectivorous *Sarracenia flava*.

RAISED VEGETABLE BEDS

One of the simplest ways to grow a few vegetables in a small garden is to use the bed system. Beds should be no more than 1.5–2m (5–6ft) wide, narrow enough to tend from pathways either side. The soil in such a small confined area can be improved to be ideal for vegetable production. Raised beds can also easily be covered with fleece if frost is forecasted. Construct them using recycled timber such as old scaffold boards or scrap decking which can be stained an appropriate colour. A depth of 15–30cm (6–12in) is adequate where there is soil underneath, but if you are constructing raised beds over concrete, 30cm (12in) would be the minimum, ideally more.

With a restricted space, choose to grow your favourites; select compact varieties and those that are sometimes called 'mini vegetables'. Use a close spacing and harvest the vegetables when small, following with successional sowings to get the most from your small space. Avoid crops which take a long time to mature, such as bulb onions and winter brassicas, and those that take up a great deal of space such as maincrop potatoes and courgettes. Otherwise there is a wide range that can be grown.

A wide range of crops can be grown in a small space. Carrots, turnips and beetroot will all produce small tender roots very quickly. Choose the leek 'Armor' for harvesting when young. Calabrese will produce small central heads at a close spacing. 'Avalanche' is a good small cauliflower and 'Minicole' a reliable compact cabbage. Tomatoes, peppers, aubergines and French beans can easily be grown in summer. Tall climbing runner beans will need a wigwam of five canes but produce attractive red flowers followed by several pickings of beans over many weeks. Salads should be sown in short rows and repeated at frequent intervals. They can be grown to maturity or harvested young as baby leaves.

Valuable crops of high quality vegetables and herbs can be grown in a small space using the raised bed technique, constructed here on top of a paved surface.

COLOUR BORDER

Planting a colour border can be great fun. There are some well known and very effective ones such as the red borders at Hidcote and the white garden at Sissinghurst.

A hot border will generally include plants in colourings of yellow, orange and red. This is a brazenly bright mix of bold colours and you can use both foliage and flower to achieve the effect. Whilst the colour range is limited, you can still get lots of different interest by choosing plants with different heights, shapes and textures. You may also choose to add in some bronze foliage, which will tone well and avoid an excess of brash colours. For example, imagine the spiky green leaves and red flowers of *Crocosmia* 'Lucifer' with the golden yellow foliage of *Choisya* 'Sundance' and a bright orange canna with broad bronze leaves such as 'Wyoming'.

If you have an empty border then you have a clean canvas on which to work, but it is more likely that you have an existing planting scheme, in which case you need to analyse what is currently present, that can remain as part of the new scheme. Start by removing those plants which obviously do not fit the brief and then see what is left and how best to fill the gaps. Don't forget that most plants, unless they are very large and well established, can usually be moved if they are not in the right place.

Sometimes a colour border, constructed with all the obvious ingredients just doesn't seem to buzz. In that situation you may have to decide whether it needs a little extra punch from something else. The hot border described above may just be waiting for a touch of rich purple, maybe some penstemon such as 'Burgundy' or 'Purple Bedder' or even the bright violet of *Geranium psilostemon*. A green border, full of lush verdant shades of green, could come alive with just a touch of white, maybe a few snowy tulips for spring and some white *Lilium regale* for midsummer. A brown border, cleverly utilizing lots of bronze foliage, together with 'Buff Beauty' roses and dark chocolate *Cosmos atrosanguineus* could be electrified with just a touch of pale blue from some *Linum perenne* or a blue agapanthus. With such colour mixes be bold, try the unthinkable and see if it works. If it doesn't you can try again next year!

HOT BORDER PLANTS

Crocosmia 'Lucifer' AGM
Hemerocallis 'Stella d'Oro'
Coreopsis verticillata 'Grandiflora' AGM
Achillea millefolium 'Paprika'
Choisya ternata 'Sundance' AGM
Helenium 'Moerheim Beauty' AGM
Canna 'Wyoming' AGM
Heuchera 'Crème Brûlée'
Penstemon 'King George'
Phormium tenax 'Bronze Baby'

Although the rich orange and red dahlias, kniphofia and persicaria are the key components of this flower border, touches of blue agapanthus and white cosmos add extra sparkle.

DEALING WITH DEEP SHADE

If you have an area of deep shade in your garden, possibly caused by a large overhanging tree, then although you have a challenge, it is not insurmountable. Don't pretend the problem isn't there by planting sun loving plants such as roses, as the result is bound to be disappointing. Work with the conditions you have got and you are likely to achieve a far greater level of success.

Initially, within the shady area try to create areas and features of interest that do not rely on living plants. Surface the soil with different types of mulch, such as gravels and cobbles, with intricately shaped boulders for extra interest. Loose materials such as these are likely to be more successful than paving, which is prone to move and crack as tree roots grow. Some people may like natural materials such as pine needles or fir cones. If possible use pale colours which will be more effective in deep shade, and highlight with features such as pieces of garden art or ceramic pots. Don't use dark colours such as deep blue, purple, bronze or maroon which will disappear without bright light to bring them to life.

There are a number of plants which will grow quite successfully in low light levels. If the shade is caused by an adjacent building or a high wall, there is no reason why you cannot plant suitable plants in the soil. However if the shade is under a large tree, then the soil is likely to be compacted, full of roots, impossible to dig and usually very dry. In this situation it is wisest to surface the area as discussed and to grow your plants in containers where you can give a good soil, plenty of feed and water. In general variegated plants do not do well in deep shade, but the list (left) includes a few real 'toughies' that will survive.

SHADE LOVING PLANTS

Fatsia japonica AGM

Aucuba japonica 'Crotonifolia' AGM

Euonymus fortunei 'Silver Queen'

Sarcococca hookeriana var. *humilis*

Mahonia aquifolium 'Apollo' AGM

Skimmia japonica 'Rubella' AGM

Gaultheria shallon

Iris foetidissima AGM

Euphorbia amygdaloides var. *robbiae* AGM

Vinca major 'Variegata' AGM

Epimedium rubrum **is a tolerant herbaceous groundcover plant that thrives in shade, giving a carpet of ruby tinted foliage and delicate crimson flowers in spring.**

A GREEN ROOF

For centuries homeowners have regarded house leeks planted on roofs as magical plants that would not only anchor loose tiles in place but also protect the home against fire and storm. In more recent times, it has become a very acceptable architectural practice to design roof structures that include carpets of green plants; these are environmentally sound keeping buildings warm in winter and cool in summer. On a small garden scale, you can take this idea and translate it to the roof of a shed, a summer house or a simple structure like a store for logs or bicycles.

The simplest of green roofs consist of a thin matting, very much like turf, which is supplied pre-planted with small species of sedum. This can be rolled out over a shed roof, anchored in place and will grow and stay green with minimal maintenance. Amazingly sedum is able to survive with almost no rooting zone. In dry weather in the summer it is inclined to go red, which is not unattractive, but then with the rains of autumn it will become lush and green again.

If you want a green roof with a greater level of interest, you can plant a range of easily grown alpine plants. Some gardeners have also had success planting roof lawns of chamomile, thyme or even small wildflower meadows. For these you will need to create a shallow planting box, filled with a suitable growing medium; this can be no more than say 5cm (2in) deep, but you will nevertheless need to be sure that the structure of your roof will take the extra weight of the soil when it is wet. Use a lightweight growing medium based on perlite. Also you must be sure that any tarred roofing felt is intact and in good condition before you cover with soil and plant it. Planted roofs will need relatively little maintenance. Some watering in very dry weather will be required, and weeding to be sure that unwanted species do not take over. Also remember that if you opt for a roof level wildflower meadow, this will need to be cut at least once a year, usually in midsummer.

PLANTS FOR A GREEN ROOF

Sedum acre 'Aureum'

Sedum spureum 'Dragon's Blood'

Sedum rupestre

Festuca glauca

Phlox subulata

Sempervivum tectorum AGM

Thymus serpyllum

Allium schoenoprasum

Armeria maritima

Hypericum polyphyllum

The roof of this log store has been embellished with a collection of sempervivum that in time will cover most of the gravel, becoming an attractive and practical feature.

GARDEN LIGHTING

If you want to use or enjoy your garden after dark, then adding lights is an enjoyable project. At the most basic, you may want to add functional illumination that will clearly show your footpaths and the edges of paved areas. But when you get beyond that, the fun starts. A visit to a garden centre will show you that there is a great selection of relatively cheap low-voltage garden lighting available to create all sorts of effects. Small spotlights can be used to highlight features, garden art or areas of planting. Spiky and architectural plants become quite dramatic with a simple low placed spotlight. You can also use the effect of shadows where you have plants with interesting shapes near a wall. In addition there are a whole host of light ropes and various twinkling lights set in strings or sheets which give different effects. White bulbs are probably the most effective, but you may like to experiment with small islands of colour.

Most garden lights work on 12v from a transformer connected to the mains electricity supply. Amazingly, although the lights are weather-proof and intended for outdoor use, the transformer often isn't. You can solve this problem with a sealed waterproof box, obtainable from an electrical supplier. In here you can fix two or more transformers together with plugs and sockets, safely away from moisture. Wires to your lights and the mains come through rubber grommets keeping the transformers and so on

dry and safe. Remember all garden electrics should be run from a proper external electric supply fitted by an electrician with a safety trip. Solar powered lights are available and the lack of cables may seem tempting, but in general they are all very underpowered. Add to this the lack of sunlight to properly recharge them in temperate areas and the result is generally disappointing.

You can also create some fun effects for special occasions using garden candles or flares which will burn giving a soft flickering light. Garden candles come on long sticks that can be poked in the soil, or you can make your own in flower pots or small lanterns. Some garden candles contain an insect deterrent which can be welcome on a summer's evening. If conditions are dry use with care and be aware of the fire risk.

Garden lighting can turn spiky plants such as this *Dasyliron longissimum* into dynamic night-time features at a relatively low cost.

FURTHER INFORMATION

HARD LANDSCAPE MATERIALS

Bradstone Suppliers of paving and hard landscape materials; the range contains some very innovative materials and surfaces such as Old Town Chelsea Cobble.
www.bradstone.com

CED Ltd UK company with many branches supplying huge range of natural stone, paving, rocks, boulders, cobbles and coloured gravels.
www.ced.ltd.uk

Haddonstone Manufacturers of a range of quality cast stone building materials and garden ornaments, mostly in heritage styles; some excellent, genuine copies of pieces from historical gardens.
www.haddonstone.com

Marshalls Manufacturers of a wide range of high quality paving usually supplied through a network of local builders' merchants and garden centres.
www.marshalls.co.uk

PLANTS

Notcutts Huge nursery producing wide range of plants with garden centres in many parts of the UK; their *Notcutts Book of Plants* is an excellent reference, particularly the blue pages that list plants suitable for many different situations and problem sites.
www.notcutts.co.uk

David Austin Roses Major grower of quality roses, in particular breeder of many of the modern New English Roses.
www.davidaustinroses.com

Rolawn Ltd Growers and suppliers of top quality cultivated lawn turf; the Medallion grade is the most suitable for most domestic lawns.
www.rolawn.co.uk

SOURCES

British Association of Landscape Industries Trade organization governing landscape contractors promoting quality design and construction. List of member contractors available.
www.bali.co.uk

Royal Horticultural Society Vast resource of information on gardens and gardening, as well as information on their own gardens open to the public.
www.rhs.org.uk

The Plant Finder On-line database, listing thousands of plants, where to obtain them in the UK and details of the nurseries supplying.
www.rhs.org.uk/rhsplantfinder

National Garden Scheme Charitable organization that arranges the opening of hundreds of large and small private gardens throughout the UK; a great starting point for inspiration and gathering ideas.
www.ngs.org.uk

DESIGN

ScapePlus Garden design and horticultural consultancy business run by Ian Cooke, garden writer and lecturer.
www.scapeplus.com

INDEX

OTHER GARDENING BOOKS FROM CROWOOD